THE OFFICIAL
TEAM
ENGLAND
WORLD CUP
SQUAD BOOK

TEAM ENGLAND • TEAM ENGLAND • TEAM ENGLAND • TEAM ENGLAND

THE OFFICIAL TEAM ENGLAND WORLD CUP SQUAD BOOK

EBURY PRESS
LONDON

1 3 5 7 9 10 8 6 4 2

First published in 1998 in Great Britain by Ebury Press, Random House, 20 Vauxhall Bridge Road, London SW1V 2SA www.randomhouse.co.uk

Random House Australia (Pty) Limited
20 Alfred Street, Milsons Point, Sydney,
New South Wales 2061, Australia

Random House New Zealand Limited
18 Poland Road, Glenfield,
Auckland 10, New Zealand

Random House South Africa (Pty) Limited
Endulini, 5A. Jubilee Road
Parktown 2193, South Africa

Random House UK Limited Reg. No. 954009

Papers used by Ebury Press are natural, recyclable products made from wood grown in sustainable forests.

Printed and bound in Great Britain by
Butler & Tanner Ltd, Frome and London

A CIP catalogue record for this book
is available from the British Library

ISBN 0-09-186440-2

Stopwatch wish to thank the Football Association,
CSS Promotions and the England Squad for their
co-operation in the production of this book.

Production Director: David Brown
Editorial Director: Barrie Gill
Art Director: Ivan Bulloch
Design Manager: Richard Langford
Designer: Julian Francis
Photographs: Allsport

The views expressed in this book are not necessarily those of
BP Oil UK Limited

CONTENTS

TEAM ENGLAND

FOREWORD

By Sally Bye, Marketing Manager, BP Oil UK

Welcome to the Official Team England World Cup Squad Book. We made it – England are going to France – and with Scotland qualifying too, 1998 promises to be an electrifying Summer for British football. Two billion football fans from every corner of the globe are eagerly anticipating the battle for the greatest prize in football. As the anticipation mounts the debates, arguments and forecasts are already raging. Will Owen dazzle on the world stage and give Ronaldo a run for his money? Will Shearer repeat his goalscoring feats of Euro '96? How will Scotland fare in that dramatic tournament opener against Brazil, who surprisingly lost against the USA? Football mania is only just beginning, the temperature is reaching fever pitch and BP is adding its support to Team England as an Official Associate. In our view, BP and England are bound to be a winning combination! This BP sponsored book is just one aspect of our support and we hope that it will add to your enjoyment of the big event. Every angle of the World Cup is covered so whether you are an ardent football fan or an armchair supporter, there will be something for you to read – from the views of captain Alan Shearer to profiles of all the key players who will be carrying our colours in France. All the important facts and fixtures are here – with a detailed look at the history of England in the World Cup to date, the battles that have taken us to France and an in-depth look at Glenn Hoddle and his staff. Their shrewd guidance could lead to massive celebrations as the tournament progresses. We hope that with your support and ours – as the Official Fuel of Team England – that our 1998 squad can emulate the glory of 1966. We will be watching and hoping. Good luck England!

NOW DO IT AGAIN!

Where were you when John Kennedy was assassinated, when a Michelin man played golf on the Moon... and when England won the World Cup?

Many of you will answer with a shake of the head simply because you were not around at the time. But the greybeards among us recall them all, especially that marvellous day at Wembley Stadium. Saturday, July 30, 1966... England 4 West Germany 2 after extra time. I remember every kick, shouting for Bobby Moore's men in a German-occupied bar on a sweltering Spanish costa.

On a black-and-white telly with a foreign commentator. It was the first day of a 'quiet family holiday' after a seemingly endless month of World Cup special editions and a final exhausting week of extra-specials. We had flown in the previous evening and I had decided to watch the match in the crowded bar just up the road. I also decided to have a double brandy every time England scored, so condemning myself to a booze-free afternoon in a hostile environment. Or so I thought. Two-and-a-half hours and four brimming brandies later, the mad Englishman emerged, stopped the roar of Spanish traffic, raced the full 800 metres of the sun-soaked beach, screaming 'We are the champions, we are the champions' before plunging fully-clothed and suicidally into the Mediterranean. I am grateful to Someone Up There for preserving me for 32 more years - but I vow here and now I shall not be responsible for my actions if England do it again. Perhaps I should settle for Brighton beach this time. So what now are England's chances? Can we truly believe the bookies who rate us in the top five? The history of 15 World Cups tells us that winning for the first time is the hardest part. Remarkably, of the mere six countries who have won the greatest prize in football, only England have failed to win it again. The prospects are daunting. Now, for the first time, 32 nations will contest the final stages. Brazil are favourites to win for the fifth time, Italy and Germany for their fourth, Argentina their third. And though England came through the qualifying stages with great credit against formidable opposition in Italy, Poland, Georgia and Moldova, there are tougher immediate hurdles ahead. There is no such thing any longer as an easy ride, and certainly not for England - as Alan Shearer points out in his specially-written article for this Team England book. Having emerged from the euphoria of the Marseille draw last December, he makes the point that England are in the only group where three of the teams were rated in the world's top ten. 'Only two can qualify,' he says, 'so in my eyes, that makes it an extremely tough group.' Having said that, we should look on the plus side and the realisation that Glenn Hoddle and Alan Shearer have the experience and temperament needed for leadership at the highest level. I am reminded of the words of Michel Platini, the great French player who is now head of the World Cup organising committee. On hearing that Hoddle had 50 or so

England caps, he said that he would have won 150 had he been a Frenchman. There is also an air of confidence coming through our section on some of the likely squad members; their opinions of one another make fascinating reading. We cannot pretend to know Hoddle's final 22. Our chosen gallery of 'likely lads', restricted as it is by printing deadlines will, one hopes, be regarded more as a tribute to those who have already played their part on the way to France. The build-up matches, starting with Cameroon, will have given the England coach and his team the opportunity to experiment and finally to mould a squad for France of enormous potential. I am indebted to

my old colleagues at Hayters for a typically professional input; to the charismatic Brian Glanville for his unique historical contribution; to Brian Woolnough for his powerful and penetrating profile of Glenn Hoddle. Also worthy of special mention is the contribution by Alec McGivan, Director of the World Cup 2006 Campaign, for his convincing presentation of England's case. As automatic qualifiers for the 2002 finals, we would surely be in with a shout!

WE HAVE A GENUINE CHANCE OF WINNING

ALAN SHEARER, back at the helm after recovering from a severe injury that threatened his career, talks frankly of England's chances of going all the way to a date in the Stade de France on July 12

Anyone who said England have got an easy draw in our World Cup group couldn't be more wrong.I didn't realise it at the time but we're in the only group where three of the teams are ranked in the world's top ten - ourselves, Colombia and Romania. Only two can qualify so, in my eyes, that makes it an extremely tough group.Yes, we are one of perhaps eight to ten countries who are going out to France believing they have a genuine chance of winning the World Cup. That's a great position to be in, but there is absolutely no way we're going to concentrate initially on anything other than securing a safe passage to the knockout stages. I'm not an expert on any of our group opponents, Colombia, Romania or Tunisia. But Glenn Hoddle and John Gorman will do their homework before June and we'll know plenty about our opponents by the time we go out to play them. Colombia are likely to field a couple of familiar names like Valderrama and my old Newcastle team-mate Faustino Asprilla. Tino was unpredictable, you really didn't know what he was going to do next on the football field but if he was firing on all cylinders, he was world-class. You could describe the Colombian team in the same way. Watch out if they are on top form. Otherwise, they can fall below those standards. I've got to hope that Tino and Colombia have an off-day when they play us! I played against Colombia at

> ‘We are in an extremely tough group and we're going to concentrate initially on securing a safe passage to the knockout stages.’

Wembley in a game best-known for goalkeeper Rene Higuita's scorpion kick rather than anything else. It was a goalless draw in a friendly so I don't think it will have too much bearing on our next meeting. Romania are a very experienced side. They qualified for the finals relatively easily and we know a couple of their players from the Premiership, most notably Dan Petrescu, of Chelsea, and Coventry's record signing Moldovan. As for Tunisia, I have never played against them. Suffice to say I leave all the homework to our management team and we'll learn about them approaching the game. I've had some great experiences in professional football but the World Cup finals will still be something special. Like any other kid in Britain, I was glued to the television during World Cup time. It is quite simply the biggest footballing event there is and when you think that only a handful of players have the opportunity of playing in a World Cup, it's going to be an experience to savour. Four years ago, I watched the finals on television from the Algarve in Portugal, where I was on holiday. Like everyone else, I was disappointed at the time we hadn't qualified. I think we've made great strides in our game since then. Everything is on the up as regards football, and the success of the national team in Euro 96 and qualifying for the World Cup is reflecting that as well. Countries like Holland, Italy, Germany, France and Argentina

will think they have a chance and we're fortunate that our recent results mean that we can quite rightly regard ourselves in the same bracket. All of the countries I mentioned, including ourselves, will be feeling that if we can put in the performances at the right time, we can go a long way. But having said that, I think Brazil are still the team to beat. They are world champions and deservedly favourites. As everyone knows, I missed the first half of 1997/98 with injury. To be honest, my first priority was to try and get fit to win my place back in the Newcastle side. But knowing the World Cup was there at the end of the season was an enormous carrot to keep working hard. I was very grateful to Glenn Hoddle and John Gorman for keeping in touch regularly while I was injured. They invited me to training sessions, England's away games and generally kept encouraging me. It was a thrill to be called up for the squad to play Chile in February. Six or seven weeks before that, I didn't think I had a chance of making that game. It was an indication of how well my recovery from the injury progressed that I was able to make the squad. Although the England players will be going to the World Cup very much focused on the task in hand, there is some time to enjoy the rest of the football. If we have time off between matches, we try and catch the games on the television. Part of you is viewing it as a professional but the other part is as a fan, simply enjoying the skills on view like any other supporters of the game.

HE'S THE BOSS IN EVERY SENSE OF THE WORD

by Brian Woolnough Chief Football Writer of The Sun and Sky TV pundit

There was not a flicker of emotion on Glenn Hoddle's face. He looked into the eyes of the media pack and said: 'We WILL qualify for the World Cup.'

It was Wednesday, February 12, 1997, and England had just lost at home to Italy. There was doom and gloom in the air. Deep down, no one thought we would now get to the finals. Except Hoddle.

He was standing on a hastily-prepared stage in the dressing-room tunnel, below the famous Wembley turf where Chelsea's little Gianfranco Zola had just stuck a dagger into English football. Hoddle, however, looked smart and unruffled in his expensive suit and answered the questions with all the confidence of a man without a care in the world.

Here then was the first real insight into Hoddle the man and, yes, Hoddle the manager. As a player he was known as 'Glenda', a marvellous talent but someone without the character to take the game by the scruff of the neck. He was also said to be injury prone, another problem that did nothing for his character reference.

So when he became England coach, we wondered if he had it in him to lead the country at the highest level of all. Did he have the knowledge and, more significantly, did he have the toughness that you need to succeed? Especially after that defeat by Italy.

From that night in 1997 he proved, without question, that he did. The Italian disaster was the turning point of his career, maybe even his life, in football. Hoddle dug deep for all the principles that had been growing in him as a player and a person.

Inner strength, real belief, confidence, single-mindedness, faith, religious feelings, they all emerged as Hoddle proved to everyone that he had what it takes.

When he went home that night after losing, he sat alone, focusing his mind on what it would take to get England to the finals. He watched a video of the game three times before falling asleep. The outcome was an unbeaten run and victory in the return game against the old enemy in Rome on October 11.

'I waited and waited for that game,' he said. 'I knew that we would qualify, I did not have any doubts. After losing at home to Italy, I knew we had to win an important away game in Poland but it did not faze me.

'I just knew we would do it. By the time Italy came, I was looking forward to the match. In the dressing-room before the game, I looked into the eyes of my players and knew before a ball was kicked that we would get the result we needed. I could sense their belief too.'

At the final whistle in Rome, Hoddle gave us a rare show of public emotion. This very private man danced and hugged his staff on the touchline, a huge smile on his face.

Belief, you see, is a key to Hoddle's life. When he was a child, he knew that one day he would be a great footballer. As an 11-year-old, he boasted that one day he would become manager of England. And, one day, he knows he is going to win the World Cup for his country.

These feelings are difficult to explain. How do you get inside a mind when the subject has always been closed? I thought he would be difficult to handle once he became England coach, stand-offish and moody, as he was at Swindon and Chelsea. Hoddle, however, changed character once he was inside Lancaster Gate. To the media he is informative and interesting, even if he does retreat into a shell, certainly behind the gate of his job.

It was as if he had got what he always wanted. The boy had been given the best toy in the shop, something that he had peered at for years and thought . . . 'if only'.

You never get really close to Hoddle because he is not that kind of person. But one or two barriers have disappeared since he took over England. The Hoddle of old would never have talked in detail about one of his players, like he did about Paul Gascoigne's domestic problems.

You never underestimate this man. Who could possibly have

known that in Rome he had the personal problems of a pending separation from wife Anne going on in his head? Here he was planning the biggest game of his career, and there were a million other things to sort out that had nothing to do with football. That, as they say, was a remarkable performance, worthy of any Oscar.

And when he returned home from Rome and all the hype and adrenalin had gone, Hoddle found himself in the living-room of his Ascot home. It was then that he finally decided to make the break as a father and husband. He does not like negatives in his life and decided that it was his marriage, and 18-year-old relationship with Anne, that had to end.

Ruthless? Certainly. But Mr Hoddle usually gets what he wants and he desperately wants to win the World Cup. This one in France in June may come too soon for him but one day, he knows he will do it.

Those kind of positive feelings are helped by Eileen Drewery, the faith-healer who has become his close friend and confidante. They met years ago when he took out her daughter and Eileen noticed that Hoddle, the young Spurs footballer, was injured. It was a hamstring strain, expected to keep him out for four weeks. She said that he would feel better in the morning and when he woke, the pain had gone and he played on the Saturday.

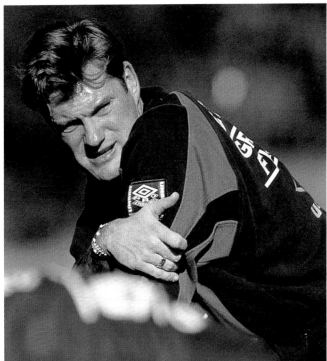

How did it happen? The young Hoddle asked and discovered that he was fascinated by these new beliefs which he began to learn about. They have been with him ever since. Every player he has managed he has encouraged to go and see Drewery if they have an injury or a personal crisis in their life that cannot be solved by more orthodox methods.

The picture of Hoddle is being painted all the time. You could certainly not call him a straightforward, ordinary bloke. He has deep passion for the game; indeed, he loves it perhaps more than anything else in his life.

Now, heading towards the World Cup, he has the nation's hopes in his hands. That is an irony in itself. The player in whom managers like Ron Greenwood and Bobby Robson never really had enough faith now carries the hopes of everyone. When Spurs were in trouble they gave the ball to Hoddle; now England have done it - and he can keep it for as long as he likes.

The FA masters are taken with him. They gave him a four-year contract when he succeeded Terry Venables and a new one will be waiting after the World Cup finals. 'We hope that he will be England manager for at least ten years,' says chairman Keith Wiseman.

'I have been tremendously impressed with him. He has enormous faith in his ability and no detail is lost in his preparation. There is also a ruthless streak and Glenn Hoddle is very much his own man. He does things his way.'

No doubt, Hoddle is his own man. As a player he knew how the game should have been played and spent many days disputing tactics with former Spurs manager Keith Burkinshaw, who now admits: 'If I could roll back the clock, I would use him differently.'

Former England manager Greenwood questioned his personality. Hoddle won 53 caps and some say it should have been 153. 'It could have been had he had a stronger personality as a man,' says Greenwood.

How different that character reference is today. You do not mix it with Mr Hoddle. He is the boss in every sense of the word. He is now playing the game exactly how he wants. 'I need my players, my team to play for me and their country with a passion,' he says.

'My players must have real belief and feeling.' Just like Hoddle has always had. He told us we would qualify and he knows that England will be successful under his control.

World Cup winners? He thinks so. Who are we to doubt him after what he has achieved against all odds? One day he will look at the media again and say: 'I told you we would do it.' Just like that night at Wembley in February.

ENGLAND FACE THREE TOUGH HURDLES

As Alan Shearer has said, there are three formidable opponents to overcome before there can be any speculation about the knockout stages.
Here CHRIS DIGHTON looks at the first-round rivals from Tunisia, Romania and Colombia.

TUNISIA

Although Tunisia were unbeaten in qualifying for only their second World Cup finals, life won't be so easy when they get down to business in France.

Their previous appearance was in Argentina back in 1978, where they surprised everyone by making a flying start, beating Mexico 3-1. They then lost to Poland 1-0 but held defending World champions West Germany to a 0-0 draw. However their results were not quite good enough to take them to the next round.

This time the environment is less hostile because the North African country has strong links with France. "It's a very balanced and top-quality group," says coach Henryk Kasperczak. "In my opinion, there's no obvious favourite and our aim is clear - to get through the first round." Kasperczak has done most of his coaching in France, playing and then leading Metz to the French Cup before having spells at Saint-Etienne, Strasbourg, Matra Racing, Montpellier and Lille. Coincidentally, he was a member of the Poland side that beat Tunisia back in 1978.

He is relying on the France-North Africa links to lift his side. "The strong popular support we should enjoy ought to help us and the first match against England in Marseille will be decisive," he says.

His leading players have made their mark with European clubs, coming to prominence in Tunisia's African Cup exploits. Adel Sellimi is still only 25 but with over 50 appearances for his country, he is Tunisia's most-capped player. A left-sided attacker with Nantes, he scored four goals in qualifying. Mehdi Ben Slimane was playing with AS Marsa in Tunisia when he went to the African Nations Cup and he was snapped up by Marseille. In 1996 he went to the German club Freiburg where Zoubier Beya, the explosive Tunisian midfielder, has made his mark. 'Zouba' was one of the players of the tournament when Tunisia reached the final of the 1996 African Nations Cup.

Tunisia's strength is that most of the rest of the world knows little about them. They performed more than well in their one previous World Cup and playing in France will be as close as they ever get to playing in a World Cup finals on their own territory. The weakness? If it goes wrong early on they could fold spectacularly.

'In my opinion, there's no obvious favourite and the first match against England in Marseille will be decisive' Tunisia's Coach

MEHDI BEN SLIMANE,
ONE OF THE STARS
OF THE TUNISIAN SQUAD
IN ACTION.

ROMANIA

Romania are a red-alert team for England, because the last time England beat them was in the World Cup of Mexico in 1970. Since then, there have been a further five meetings of the two countries with four draws and one Romanian win.

Coached until February 1998 by the deeply-religious Anghel Iordanescu - a player and then coach with Steaua Bucharest - Romania scored an impressive 37 goals in 10 qualifying matches and conceded a miserly four.

"I wanted to play the top teams right from the first round to get into the swing of things, so I've got my wish," says Iordanescu. "This isn't an easy group and we'll be shooting for second place at the very least - a target in keeping with what we showed we could do in the last World Cup in America."

Iordanescu was surprisingly replaced four months before the finals by Victor Piturca, the former under-21 team coach and ex-Steaua striker. In Italia 1990, they reached the last 16 where they were beaten 5-4 on penalties by the Republic of Ireland; four years ago they went one round better where again, they were undone by their failure in the penalty shoot-out. This time they drew 2-2 with Sweden in normal time and lost the shoot-out 5-4. Romania may be a poor country but their leading players have roamed the world to find fame and fortune. The best-known to England followers will be Dan Petrescu, the Chelsea player who has blossomed as a wing-back; dangerous going forward, strong at the back.

How ironic that Glenn Hoddle - at the time the Chelsea manager - was the man responsible for shaping Petrescu, who has also played for Steaua Bucharest and Italian Serie A sides Foggia and Genoa. The other well-known Romanian is Gheorghi Hagi, now plying his trade in Turkey with Galatasaray. France 98 will be his swansong and as Mick McCarthy, the Republic of Ireland manager, remembers from Italia 90, the only time he got near Hagi was to swap shirts at the end of the game. "He's the best I've played against," says McCarthy.

True to the Romanian wandering gypsy spirit is goalkeeper Bogdan Stela, now with Steaua Bucharest. He has earned a living in four other countries, playing in Spain for Mallorca, Belgium with Standard Liege, Austria and Rapid Vienna and Turkey with Samsunspor.

He will be a key player and needs to shed the down-side of his reputation - for making blinding saves followed by colossal clangers. He could be the weakness for a Romanian side that otherwise looks alarmingly well-balanced.

VIOREL MOLDOVAN, IN ACTION WITH ROMANIA, IS A NEW FAVOURITE OF COVENTRY CITY FANS.

'I wanted to play the top teams from the first round... and we'll be shooting for second place at the very least.' EX-ROMANIAN COACH

COLOMBIA

Infamously tipped by Pele as "the dark horses" in America for the 1994 World Cup, Colombia proceeded to make the world's greatest footballer look foolish as they succumbed in a tragic comedy of errors. First they were hammered 3-1 by Romania, then lost 2-1 to USA after Andres Escobar scored a bizarre own-goal. Escobar was subsequently shot dead when he returned to Colombia, prompting talk of a betting coup soured by Colombia's abysmal performance. Certainly memories of the killing will leave an incentive of fear this time around as Colombia head to France with several of the same exotic stars of 1994, including Faustino Asprilla, the man who warmed many a cold Tyne night with his performances for Newcastle United.

The distinctive Carlos Valderrama, the man with the red-head, Afro hair-style that looks like Moses' blazing bush, will be playing his third and final World Cup finals. Valderrama has won more than 100 caps for his country and is one of the genuine characters of the world game, blessed with sublime midfield skills and a sense of timing that cannot be beaten. He refuses to see his final outing as the end of an era. "People like the way I play and I'm not going to change that now," he says. "But Colombia are not going to fall apart when I retire. There are a lot of good young players who can replace me." Coach Hernan Dario Gomez was appointed after USA 94. The right-hand man to Francisco Maturana for that trip, Gomez has brought the side through a long qualifying process of 15 matches and inspired them to pick up their game after a run of three defeats in February and April 1997 - by Argentina, Paraguay and Peru - which threatened to derail their drive for France. In the end Colombia won eight, lost four and drew three in a qualifying marathon which started back in April 1996. To progress further this time (and avenge that defeat by Romania), the leading Colombian players will need to hit top form early.

British football followers know that Asprilla can play and he will need to repeat regularly the sort of form which brought him a hat-trick in a 4-1 win over Chile. In fact, he was Colombia's leading scorer in qualifying with seven goals. Freddy Rincon is another experienced head and has had spells in both Italy (Napoli) and Spain (Real Madrid) but prefers football in Brazil because, as he says: "You can enjoy yourself more on the field."

France will be Colombia's fourth visit to the World Cup finals - the first was in 1962 - and only in 1990 in Italy have they gone past the first stage. Then they beat the United Arab Emirates 2-0 and the draw that followed with West Germany was enough to take them through to uncharted waters - the last 16. There they faced one of the emerging African giants, Cameroon. In the end Colombia were beaten 2-1 in extra time.

This time Colombia's strength will be recent experience and the maturity of key players like Rincon and Valderrama. Against that has to be balanced the strain of a South American team travelling to Europe and they must stand firm when things go wrong on the pitch.

'Colombia are not going to fall apart when I retire. There are a lot of good, young players who can replace me.' CARLOS VALDERRAMA

LA ROUTE POUR FRANCE

England fought their way through a veritable minefield of enemy opposition to head their qualifying group for the finals in France. Here we recall those eight nerve-tingling tussles.

September 1, 1996

Moldova 0 England 3

Chisinau

Glenn Hoddle's first game as England coach brought a comforting result for the 750 fans who paid £259 for a day trip to a new country carved out of the old Russia. England's early jitters were calmed by two goals midway through the first half. New boy David Beckham started the move that ended with Nick Barmby thumping in Gary Neville's cross after 23 minutes. Two minutes later, Paul Gascoigne's looping shot found the net after Paul Ince and Barmby's neat approach work. But the biggest grin of the game came from Alan Shearer. Neville and Gareth Southgate linked up for Shearer to score England's third goal after 61 minutes. Hoddle's side had begun the long march to their first World Cup finals since Gascoigne's tears of 1990. Shearer looked back on the game with warm memories, delighted to mark his first game as skipper with his eleventh international goal. He said: "Obviously it was a great thrill for me. The pitch was diabolical and meant we had to play the game at training pace, which didn't suit us, but we came away satisfied. If you had said before that game we would win 3-0, we would have said 'yes, we'll take that'."

Two goals from Alan Shearer - who else? - kept England on the road to France. But this was a bumpy ride against a Polish side that were a goal up in six minutes and looking likely to get another. But by half-time England were ahead and hanging on. First, Shearer challenged Polish goalkeeper Andrzej Wozinak to head Glenn Hoddle's men level after 25 minutes, then 12 minutes later he smashed in the second after a link with Newcastle teammate Les Ferdinand. David Seaman had several saves to make in the second half but when the final whistle went, England were clutching three points and the fans were saluting Shearer. Their feelings were echoed by Hoddle, who said: "Alan will always score goals in so many different ways - spectaculars, headers, tap-ins. He is a player both respected and envied. There has been a levelling-out of teams and the difference will be a player like Alan, like Paolo Rossi, like Jurgen Klinsmann. He puts fear into the opposition even if he's not on his best form." It wasn't a convincing England performance to mark Hoddle's first Wembley game in charge and he admitted there were "a few stern words" at half-time. But the Poles had proved Italy weren't the only dangerous side in this group.

What a start! The action in Moldova (far left) produced a three-goal bonus, followed by a double strike against Poland by the rampaging Shearer (left).

'He puts fear into the opposition even if he's not on his best form' HODDLE ON SHEARER

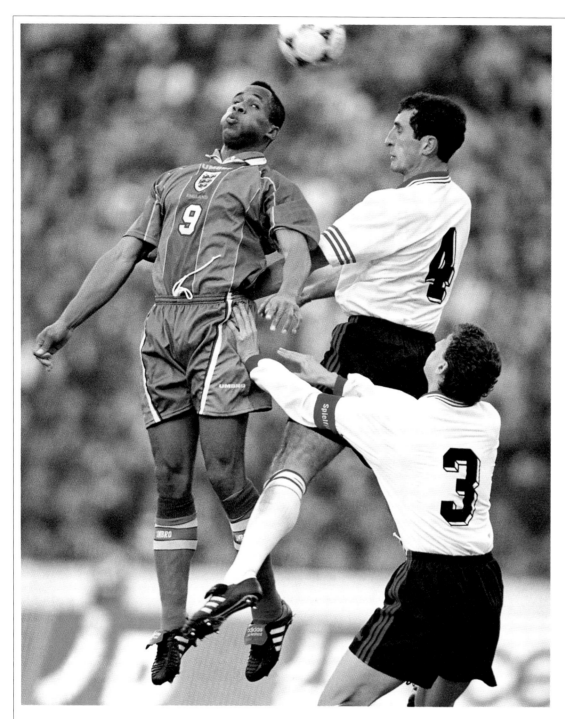

England's strikers on the rampage, with Les Ferdinand heading for the heights in Georgia (left) and Alan Shearer at full speed (right) against Italy at Wembley.

Georgi Kinkladze was the name to fear when England stepped out against Georgia. But a tremendous all-round performance wiped out the niggling doubts of England's first two qualifying games and left Kinkladze a baffled spectator for most of the match. This was the kind of collective England display that Glenn Hoddle had been urging on his side and the England coach had been brave enough to take a massive gamble on Paul Gascoigne. He stuck with the Rangers star despite Gascoigne's well-publicised domestic problems, warned him to play with head instead of heart and had that faith rewarded. Gascoigne said: "I knew there was a lot of pressure on Glenn when he stood by me. If things hadn't gone well he would have taken the flak. I like to think I repaid him." Certainly Gascoigne was involved in both England goals. He began the first with a clever through-ball to Les Ferdinand, who put Teddy Sheringham in for a shot that went in off a defender. The second goal confirmed England's dominance of a game that left David Seaman a lonely figure. Gascoigne and Sheringham exchanged passes to give Ferdinand the chance to score from just inside the penalty area. This was an impressive performance. They were solid at the back with Sol Campbell making his first international start and lively in midfield where David Batty, Paul Ince and Gascoigne worked non-stop, while Sheringham and Ferdinand confirmed that, even without Shearer, England could still score goals.

This was England's first World Cup defeat at Wembley in 48 years, yet Glenn Hoddle insisted: "It's a disappointment but not a disaster. There is no way we are out of this competition." Yet disaster seemed the right word to most of the thousands of England fans meandering miserably from the ground. Realistically, one team stood between England and a place in the World Cup finals - Italy. Their victory at Wembley made them favourites to qualify and left England facing a massive challenge. Hoddle's problems had started before the match. David Seaman was out with a knee injury and Tony Adams was missing too. The England coach gambled. First, he surprised many by giving Seaman's job to Ian Walker of Spurs and then he chose out-of-form Matt Le Tissier to inspire his country. Sadly it didn't work. By the time Le Tissier was substituted after 60 minutes, England were a goal down and struggling. That goal was scored after 18 minutes by Zola, who had swapped the blue of Chelsea for the azure of Italy. It came from a characteristic Italian strike on the break. Le Tissier was caught, Alessandro Costacurta fed Zola and he ran on to fire a shot inside Walker's near post despite a despairing challenge from Sol Campbell. Le Tissier, who went close with a first-half header, revealed later: "If that had gone in the headlines would have been very different. I've spoken to Glenn since and he's told me that, watching the video of the match, he thought I looked the player most likely to score and that he now feels he should have kept me on a little longer." For Zola there were no regrets. He said of his goal: "It was a wonderful moment. To score a goal like this, especially against England at Wembley, is what I dreamed about as a small boy."

'A disappointment but not a disaster. There is no way we're out' HODDLE AFTER WEMBLEY

It's that magic moment in Rome when England can say we did it! Now at last, the blood-stained and battle-scarred captain Paul Ince can seal it with a kiss.

The chase to catch Italy was on. Zola and his teammates had been held to a draw by Poland earlier in the month so the gap was down to two points. It was still two after England's Wembley win because at the same time the Italians were beating Poland in their return match in Naples. David Seaman and Tony Adams were back in the side but this was an England team grinding out a result rather than putting on a show. Teddy Sheringham scored just before half-time and it was a cracker. Alan Shearer took a long ball from Graeme Le Saux down the left and whacked over a cross for Sheringham to head in. But there was little else to cheer and a lot for Glenn Hoddle to worry about until an England free-kick on the edge of the area with just a minute to go.

Sheringham pushed the ball back and Shearer sent a savage shot into the far top corner of the net. There were bonuses beyond the three points, especially the imposing form of Sol Campbell in defence. His man-of-the match show wiped out some of the heartache of the Italy game. Campbell said: "That was the best I had played for England. I was blamed against Italy but the win over Georgia was a much more solid performance and it was encouraging to play my part."

'I was blamed against Italy but this win over Georgia was the best I had played' SOL CAMPBELL

May 31, 1997

Poland 0 England 2

Chorzow

Glenn Hoddle acknowledged the most testing victory of his short reign with a leap of celebration. England had arrived in Chorzow to face a side that had worried them at Wembley and were themselves still in with a chance of making the finals. By the final whistle, England had added to their blossoming reputation with goals from Alan Shearer and Teddy Sheringham. It wasn't pretty but it was effective, the first England win in Poland since Alf Ramsey's side of 1966. Alan Shearer put England ahead after just six minutes with his fifth World Cup goal in the 1998 qualifiers. Robert Lee started the move and Paul Ince produced a superb final pass. But just before half-time, Shearer missed a penalty and it wasn't until the final minute that Lee cut the ball across goal for Sheringham to sweep it in. Four years previously in Poland, Ince had been labelled a headless chicken by the then England manager Graham Taylor. Ince said: "At the time some people might have thought Graham Taylor was right. I didn't. But we have come a long way since then."

Shearer's last-minute blast is too good for the jam-packed Georgia defence (opposite), while Ince strives to keep England's defence intact in the return match with Poland.

An extraordinary night! It began with a moving candlelit minute of remembrance for Diana, Princess of Wales, and ended with a national celebration as a Paul Gascoigne-inspired England destroyed Moldova, while group rivals Italy were being held to a goalless draw in Georgia. Gascoigne was once again the maestro, with two-goal Ian Wright and Paul Scholes his able lieutenants. Scholes scored first with a diving header from David Beckham's cross. A minute after half-time, Gascoigne ran at a retreating defence to feed Wright the chance to make it 2-0. Then Wright was the provider as he played in Gascoigne with a neat one-two for the third goal after 80 minutes and, just before full-time, Wright seized on Stan Collymore's pass for his second goal and England's fourth. The Arsenal striker said: "It was an emotional night." And for Gascoigne it was a night to cherish. He said: "I couldn't have been happier with the way it went. That was one of my best performances for England." His teammates agreed. Les Ferdinand said: "People might say it was only Moldova, but put Gazza against anyone in that form and he'll cause them problems all night long. He was fantastic." David Beckham said: "When you see him doing things like that, he inspires everyone who is playing around him. He talks to me throughout the game and helps me." Gascoigne and his England teammates came off the pitch to hear of Italy's draw in Georgia and knew then that a draw in the final game in Rome would take them to the finals in France. The mood in the camp was confident.

'Gazza in that form will cause problems all night long against anyone. He was fantastic' LES FERDINAND

'Gascoigne told him he looked like a pint of Guinness but this night was all about stout English hearts' TRIBUTE TO PAUL INCE

Action man Paul Scholes (far left) found the Wembley net against Moldova, while Paul Ince (left) remained bloody and defiant against the Italians' siege in Rome.

October 11, 1997

Italy 0 England 0

Rome

Paul Ince summed it up. White-bandaged head, bloodied shirt and a broad grin. Paul Gascoigne told him he looked like a pint of Guinness but this night was all about stout English hearts rather than Irish stout. Glenn Hoddle's side had arrived knowing that a draw would take them to the World Cup finals and they got it. It wasn't pretty. England had Tony Adams, Gareth Southgate and Sol

Campbell unyielding at the back. David Batty played the game of his life in midfield along with Ince, who needed six stitches in his gashed head. Up front, Ian Wright waged a one-man war. No visiting team had managed a point in 15 previous World Cup matches in Rome. England did it and could even have won. Wright hit the post from a narrow angle in the last minute and Sheringham missed the rebound. Drama over? Not quite. For Italy struck back immediately, a cross came in and Christian Vieri had a free header at David Seaman's goal. The whole stadium held its breath and the ball flew wide. England had their point

and, what's more, the confidence to go into France '98 believing they can win it. Seaman said: "There is a positive and confident atmosphere among the players. You saw that in the way we played against Italy." And Graeme Le Saux added: "We showed we were able to handle pressure. Tony Adams said the atmosphere against Italy was the most intense we have ever faced and we handled it brilliantly." Ince was captain for the night, but he knew where the credit lay. "There have never been any doubts in Glenn Hoddle's mind that we would qualify. He drummed it into us and he was right."

SPOTLIGHT ON THE STARS

Ronaldo
Brazil

RONALDO LUIZ NAZARIO DA LIMA

BORN: RIO DE JANEIRO, BRAZIL

AGE: 21

CLUB: INTER MILAN

PREVIOUS CLUBS: CRUZEIRO [BRAZIL], PSV EINDHOVEN, BARCELONA

Ronaldo already has a World Cup winners medal as a 17-year-old on the Brazilian bench in 1994. Now he wants the real thing. Ronaldo says modestly: "I have an idea who is the greatest striker in the world, but I will keep it to myself." England's Alan Shearer, though, harbours a few doubts. He says: "It will be interesting to see how Ronaldo copes with all the attention and publicity that will surround him and Brazil." Ronaldo took just 29 games to score his first 20 international goals and has lived up to all the hype that accompanied his £27million move from Barcelona to Inter Milan. He has become Serie A's most complete striker. Former England manager Bobby Robson, who took Ronaldo from PSV Eindhoven to Barcelona, says: "The kid can pick the ball up on the halfway line, turn and, whatever's ahead of him, he can just go through them and finish."

OF WORLD SOCCER

Schmeichel
Denmark

PETER BOLESHAW SCHMEICHEL

BORN: GLADSAXE

AGE: 34

CLUB: MANCHESTER UNITED

PREVIOUS CLUB: BRONDBY

The 6ft 4in goalkeeper has won four English championships and two FA Cups since moving to Manchester United from Brondby in the summer of 1991 for a modest £650,000. Schmeichel won his 97th cap for Denmark in a goalless draw in Greece, the game which clinched qualification for France '98. He is the ultimate perfectionist and his Danish teammates draw straws to decide who gives him shooting practice. The losers know that they will be out on the training pitch far longer than the rest of the squad. United manager Alex Ferguson says simply: "He's a winner. It takes him days to get over a defeat and there are not many Europeans like that." There is a hidden side to the giant Dane. He inherited a passion for music from his father, and says: "I use music to relax and try to play a bit on the piano before every game. Anything from Billy Joel to classical."

Asprilla
Colombia

Hinestroza Faustino Hernan Asprilla

Born: Tulua

Age: 27

Club: Parma

Previous clubs: Atletico Nacional de Medellin, Cueuta Deportivo, Parma, Newcastle United

Newcastle United fans were stunned by Asprilla's sudden move back to Parma, but the memories linger on. One night in particular stands out, a thrilling 3-2 European Champions League win over Barcelona. Asprilla scored all three goals, celebrated with three of his trademark handstands and the adulation poured down from the terraces. The Colombians call Asprilla 'The Octopus'. His lanky-legged style sometimes makes him look ungainly, but it can't disguise the enormous talent that will make him a real dangerman in the World Cup finals. His former Tyneside teammate Robert Lee says: "Right from the first time he met us, he was immensely popular. He is a genuinely funny man, and the more English he acquired the funnier he became. Obviously, Tino is extremely gifted; however, his enthusiasm for Newcastle waned once Parma were in touch. His move to them had an air of inevitability about it."

'His lanky-legged style sometimes makes him look ungainly but he has enormous talent'

Batistuta
Argentina

Gabriel Omar Batistuta

Born: Reconquista, Sante Fe

Age: 29

Club: Fiorentina

Previous clubs: Boca Juniors, River Plate

Arguments rage about who is the best striker in the world. Ronaldo or Batistuta? Ronaldo may have the potential, but Batistuta has the experience. The Argentinian has been one of the most consistent performers in Serie A, scoring more than 100 goals since joining Fiorentina in 1991 and fulfilling the prediction of Diego Maradona, who insisted: "Gabriel is certain to become a success in Italy." Batistuta has aroused interest from a number of Premiership clubs, most notably Liverpool, Newcastle and Manchester United - all of whom have been linked with the striker. Only disagreement over personal terms has so far prevented a spell in England, which is a shame as the striker is Cantona-like, especially in his attitude, often insisting he would rather talk about cinema, music or politics than football and regularly criticising the consumer society. He is a keen Formula 1 motor-racing fan. He was a member of the Argentina team that disappointed in USA four years ago, and will be keen to make up for that in what will probably be his last World Cup appearance.

'Who is the world's best? Ronaldo may have the potential but Batistuta has the experience'

Mijatovic
Yugoslavia

PREDRAG MIJATOVIC

BORN: PODGORICA

AGE: 29

CLUB: REAL MADRID

PREVIOUS CLUBS: PARTIZAN BELGRADE, VALENCIA

Mijatovic first came to attention after signing for Valencia in 1993. He was an unknown when he arrived, but he didn't remain so for long, developing into one of the most impressive players in Spain, and helping the club to the league runners-up spot. He is blessed with fierce pace as well as excellent control. His subsequent transfer to Real Madrid for £6.3 million caused some resentment among Valencia fans, who felt their idol had deserted them. But as Mijatovic pointed out: "Football provides a short career so you have to take advantage of your best years. Anyway, it's not about money but success. I came to Real Madrid to win things. I won't be satisfied if I don't win at least two titles and and the European Cup." Mijatovic is certainly not short of ambition and has also been quoted as saying: "I have been the best player in Spain, now I want to be European Footballer of the Year." He will have a chance to stake his claim this summer.

Suker
Croatia

DAVOR SUKER

BORN: OSIJEK

AGE: 30

CLUB: REAL MADRID

PREVIOUS CLUBS: OSIJEK, CROATIA ZAGREB, SEVILLE

Davor Suker has already been a World Cup winner, and has even had the honour of being the top scorer in the competition. Back in 1987 he was part of the Yugoslav team which lifted the Junior World Cup. Nine years later, he came to England for Euro '96 having scored more goals than any other player in qualifying. He then wowed everybody with a beautifully lobbed effort which left Peter Schmeichel baffled. His international record is outstanding at almost a goal a game, and he also contributes to the national team's finances by arranging all their sponsorship and advertising deals. Manchester United have inquired, Newcastle United have begged and Arsenal have had talks. Croatian coach Miroslav Blazevic says: "There is no greater genius in football."

Enrique
Spain

LUIS ENRIQUE MARTINEZ GARCIA

BORN: ASTURIAS

AGE: 27

CLUB: BARCELONA

PREVIOUS CLUBS: SPORTING GIJON, REAL MADRID

In a Barcelona team which boasted Ronaldo among its number, Luis Enrique was voted 'most valuable player' by the Nou Camp fans. The man judged more useful than the world's most expensive player cost the Spanish side absolutely nothing. He spent five years and won a Spanish title with Real Madrid, but they dithered about his contract. Barca stepped in and they snapped up one of the world's most versatile

and spirited midfielders. "It's a real luxury having a player like Luis," says former Barcelona manager Bobby Robson. "Not only can he play in just about every position, but his enthusiasm and will to win are contagious. His attitude is always 100 per cent commitment." Four years ago, Enrique was in the World Cup headlines when he was the victim of an horrendous tackle by Italy's Mauro Tassotti, but the chances are that there will be more plaudits than pity in France. Spanish manager Javier Clemente says: "When he plays like he can, he is just unstoppable."

Bergkamp
Holland

DENNIS BERGKAMP

BORN: AMSTERDAM

AGE: 28

CLUB: ARSENAL

PREVIOUS CLUBS: AJAX, INTER MILAN

The hot-shot Arsenal striker hit some of the best form of his career during the 1997-98 Premiership season, his third and by far the most fruitful with the north London club. He was signed by Bruce Rioch for £7.5million from Inter Milan in 1995 and there were doubts that the Dutchman would cope with the constant physical nature of the English game. Such doubts, however, were based on wishful thinking by his opponents. Bergkamp, christened Dennis because his father was a Manchester United fan whose idol was Denis Law, has proved a deadly finisher for his country with more than 30 goals so far. Not even a fear of flying can hold him back. "The guy produces stuff on the training ground that takes your breath away," says David Seaman, the England goalkeeper. "He can shoot with so much power without any backlift - and that's a real talent."

'He has always scored spectacular goals but is far more than just a goalscorer'

Zidane
France

ZINEDINE ZIDANE

BORN: MARSEILLE

AGE: 25

CLUB: JUVENTUS

PREVIOUS CLUBS: CANNES, BORDEAUX

Much rests on the shoulders of Zinedine Zidane but that will not bother the attacking Juventus midfielder. He marked his international debut with two late goals as France came from 2-0 down to draw with the Czech Republic in 1995 and has been setting a good example ever since. Zidane has become the modern French hero and after joining Bordeaux in 1992, he was voted France's young player of the year. During the 1995-96 season, he played more games than any other French player and by the time of Euro '96 was looking tired. Even so, Juventus could see he was worth his weight in gold and duly made their move. The Italians have gone for a strongly-influenced French midfield where Zidane is linked up with Didier Deschamps. Zidane has been scoring spectacular goals throughout his career but is far more than a goalscorer. Alex Ferguson, whose Manchester United side have faced Juventus several times in the last two seasons, has watched the Frenchman's progress with interest. "I regard him more as a front player, but at Juventus he's in central midfield. You can see he has developed the ability that was always there." England and Manchester United striker Teddy Sheringham also rates Zidane as one of the best.

Carlos
Brazil

ROBERTO CARLOS

BORN: SAO PAULO

AGE: 25

CLUB: INTER MILAN

PREVIOUS CLUBS: SAO JOAO, PALMEIRAS

Roberto Carlos came second behind Ronaldo in FIFA's World Player of the Year award for 1997, but he is best remembered for his astonishing swerving free-kick against France in Le Tournoi in the summer of 1997. It was a goal which Carlos insists was no fluke. He says: "There was nothing lucky about it. I work 50 minutes a day on my free-kicks and have practised them for years." But the latest Brazilian dead-ball king has more than one string to his bow. An accomplished defender, he plays left back for Brazil and earned his first cap at the age of 18. He has long been a target of Premiership clubs, with Arsenal and Liverpool both trying to buy him before Inter Milan stepped in. Among his many fans is Stuart Pearce, another defender who has been known to take the odd free-kick. Pearce admits: "After seeing Roberto's effort against France, a number of us tried it during England training the next day. Let's just say we lost more than a few balls down the motorway."

'I work 50 minutes a day on my free-kicks and have practised them for years'

Klinsmann
Germany

JURGEN KLINSMANN

BORN: GOPPINGEN

AGE: 33

CLUB: TOTTENHAM

PREVIOUS CLUBS: STUTTGART KICKERS, VFB STUTTGART, INTER MILAN, MONACO, TOTTENHAM, BAYERN MUNICH, SAMPDORIA

This will be Klinsmann's final fling. His goals helped Germany to World Cup triumph in 1990 and European Championship victory in 1996. Now he says he will retire from international football after these finals, but it will not dim an appetite for goals that in a nomadic career has made him a success at most of his clubs. Klinsmann helped Stuttgart to the 1989 Uefa Cup final, where they lost to Napoli, then joined Inter Milan and scored 13 goals in his first season in Serie A. He signed up for Tottenham after the 1994 World Cup, formed a devastating partnership with Teddy Sheringham and was voted Footballer of the Year. At the end of the season, however, he fell out with Spurs' chairman Alan Sugar and went to Bayern Munich, before returning to White Hart Lane via Sampdoria. In between times, he led Germany to success in Euro '96 in England. "The thing about Klinsmann is that he has always been a big-game player with a great attitude," says Alex Ferguson, the Manchester United manager. "He has that aura, that style, that experience."

Del Piero
Italy

ALESSANDRO DEL PIERO

BORN: CONEGLIANO NEAR TREVISO

AGE: 23

CLUB: JUVENTUS

PREVIOUS CLUB: AC PADUA

Juventus are far from the most sentimental of clubs when it comes to retaining players, but they kept faith with Del Piero in the summer of 1997. The youngster did not have the best of times the previous season, and rumours of too much time spent on the dance floor started to circulate. The fact that he stayed and others went gave a clear signal from Juventus that Del Piero was their man, their future. Del Piero was nicknamed "Pinturrichio" after a 16th century Italian Renaissance painter following a cheeky "artistic" backheel that brought a goal in the 3-1 Champions' Cup defeat by Borussia Dortmund in 1997. His international career is in its infancy but defences know the threat he carries. "He's a difficult player to face," says David Beckham, the Manchester United and England midfielder. "He's very tricky and you have to keep your wits about you - a real challenge." Like Beckham, Del Piero is an expert with the dead-ball and he has an instinctive ball control to go with his natural flair. No wonder Italy are excited by him.

Raul
Spain

RAUL GONZALEZ BLANCO

BORN: MADRID

AGE: 20

CLUB: REAL MADRID

PREVIOUS CLUB: ATLETICO MADRID

How Atletico Madrid must regret scrapping their youth policy. That decision by club president Jesus Gil may have saved the club a few pesetas in the short term, but it lost them the services of Spain's most exciting player. Raul was among the youngsters dumped by the club. He immediately switched allegiance to Real, where he is now the star player, tied to a contract worth some £12 million. In fact, such has been the striker's impact in his first few seasons, some fans have taken to calling the team Raul Madrid. He made his debut for the club at 17 years and four months, after just one reserve game. He immediately made an impression in the first team, scoring one and setting up two more in a 3-0 win over Atletico. Within a year he was playing for his country and the best of his career is surely yet to come. Spain's coach Javier Clemente says: "Raul is destined to make his mark on a whole generation, and not just in Spanish football. But at his age, he's got to take things one step at a time."

Salas
Chile

MARCELO SALAS

BORN: TEMUCO

AGE: 23

CLUB: RIVER PLATE

PREVIOUS CLUB: UNIVERSIDAD DE CHILE

Marcelo Salas and his on-off transfer to Manchester United frequently filled the sports pages in the first few months in late 1997. The deal eventually fell through but not before Alex Ferguson had flown out to Argentina to watch the prolific striker in action. "I think he could play in this country without any problem," was the United manager's verdict. "He is a goalscorer and a very good player. Everyone is interested in players like him." Bad news for United, Salas will join Lazio on a seven-year contract after the World Cup. He has already become an automatic choice up front for Chile and delighted fans with a first-half hat-trick in the 4-1 victory over Colombia. He also scored in the 3-0 win over Bolivia that secured Chile's place at France '98. Every World Cup produces new international stars and, this time, Salas could be the name that rings round the world. England fans had a close-up of his scoring talents when he got the goals in Chile's 2-0 Wembley win in February 1998.

Okocha
Nigeria

AUGUSTINE 'JAY JAY' OKOCHA

BORN: LAGOS

AGE: 24

CLUB: FENERBAHCE

PREVIOUS CLUBS: BLACK ROCKS, ENUGU RANGERS, NEUNKIRCHEN, EINTRACHT FRANKFURT, BORUSSIA DORTMUND

Okocha has packed a lot in for a relative youngster. He already has experience of a World Cup, having played in the Nigerian side that reached the last 16 in America 1994. He also won an Olympic gold medal with the under-23 Nigerian team that stood on the podium in Atlanta in 1996. Okocha is a creative, stylish and unpredictable midfielder who starred in Fenerbahce's win against Manchester United at Old Trafford in the Champions League. After proving a success in the German Bundesliga, he has taken to life in Turkey with the Istanbul giants, applying for Turkish citizenship and changing his name to Muhammed Yavuz Okocha. No less a judge than Michel Platini has tipped him to be the player of the tournament. He recently married in Lagos, the Nigerian capital.

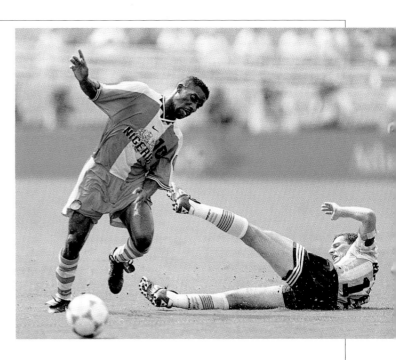

Djorkaeff
France

YOURI DJORKAEFF

BORN: LYON

AGE: 30

CLUB: INTER MILAN

PREVIOUS CLUBS: GRENOBLE, STRASBOURG, MONACO, PARIS ST GERMAIN

Djorkaeff is following in the family footsteps by appearing in the World Cup finals - father Jean was France's full back in the 1966 tournament in England. But even dad must admit that Djorkaeff junior could have a far bigger impact this time than he ever did. Djorkaeff is the closest France have had to Michel Platini since the midfield maestro set up and scored goals in the 1984 European Championship. Djorkaeff must have learned by playing alongside Ronaldo with Inter Milan this season. His Inter colleague from last term, Paul Ince, says: "This guy has great skill and a very good footballing brain." Djorkaeff was voted French Player of the Year in 1996 and will be seeking to make amends for a poor Euro '96.

FIRST-ROUND SCORECARD

GROUP A

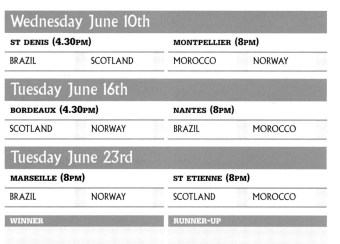

🇧🇷 **BRAZIL** ✕ **SCOTLAND**

NORWAY ★ **MOROCCO**

Wednesday June 10th

ST DENIS (4.30PM)		MONTPELLIER (8PM)	
BRAZIL	SCOTLAND	MOROCCO	NORWAY

Tuesday June 16th

BORDEAUX (4.30PM)		NANTES (8PM)	
SCOTLAND	NORWAY	BRAZIL	MOROCCO

Tuesday June 23rd

MARSEILLE (8PM)		ST ETIENNE (8PM)	
BRAZIL	NORWAY	SCOTLAND	MOROCCO

WINNER	RUNNER-UP

GROUP B

ITALY **CHILE**

★ **CAMEROON** **AUSTRIA**

Thursday June 11th

BORDEAUX (4.30PM)		TOULOUSE (8PM)	
ITALY	CHILE	CAMEROON	AUSTRIA

Wednesday June 17th

ST ETIENNE (4.30PM)		MONTPELLIER (8PM)	
CHILE	AUSTRIA	ITALY	CAMEROON

Tuesday June 23rd

ST DENIS (3PM)		NANTES (3PM)	
ITALY	AUSTRIA	CHILE	CAMEROON

WINNER	RUNNER-UP

GROUP C

FRANCE **SOUTH AFRICA**

SAUDI ARABIA **DENMARK**

Friday June 12th

LENS (4.30PM)		MARSEILLE (8PM)	
SAUDI ARABIA	DENMARK	FRANCE	SOUTH AFRICA

Thursday June 18th

TOULOUSE (4.30PM)		ST DENIS (8PM)	
SOUTH AFRICA	DENMARK	FRANCE	SAUDI ARABIA

Wednesday June 24th

LYON (3PM)		BORDEAUX (3PM)	
FRANCE	DENMARK	SOUTH AFRICA	SAUDI ARABIA

WINNER	RUNNER-UP

GROUP D

SPAIN **NIGERIA**

PARAGUAY **BULGARIA**

Friday June 12th / Saturday June 13th

MONTPELLIER (1.30PM)		NANTES (1.30PM)	
PARAGUAY	BULGARIA	SPAIN	NIGERIA

Friday June 19th

PARIS (4.30PM)		ST ETIENNE (8PM)	
NIGERIA	BULGARIA	SPAIN	PARAGUAY

Wednesday June 24th

LENS (8PM)		TOULOUSE (8PM)	
SPAIN	BULGARIA	NIGERIA	PARAGUAY

WINNER	RUNNER-UP

GROUP E

 HOLLAND    BELGIUM

 SOUTH KOREA    MEXICO

Saturday June 13th

LYON (4.30PM)		ST DENIS (8PM)	
SOUTH KOREA	MEXICO	HOLLAND	BELGIUM

Saturday June 20th

BORDEAUX (4.30PM)		MARSEILLE (8PM)	
BELGIUM	MEXICO	HOLLAND	SOUTH KOREA

Thursday June 25th

ST ETIENNE (3PM)		PARIS (3PM)	
HOLLAND	MEXICO	BELGIUM	SOUTH KOREA
WINNER		**RUNNER-UP**	

GROUP F

 GERMANY   USA

 YUGOSLAVIA   IRAN

Sunday June 14th		Monday June 15th	
ST ETIENNE (4.30PM)		**PARIS (8PM)**	
YUGOSLAVIA	IRAN	GERMANY	USA

Sunday June 21st			
LENS (1.30PM)		**LYON (8PM)**	
GERMANY	YUGOSLAVIA	USA	IRAN

Thursday June 25th			
MONTPELLIER (8PM)		**NANTES (8PM)**	
GERMANY	IRAN	USA	YUGOSLAVIA
WINNER		**RUNNER-UP**	

GROUP G

 ROMANIA    COLUMBIA

 ENGLAND    TUNISIA

Monday June 15th

MARSEILLE (1.30PM)		LYON (4.30PM)	
ENGLAND	TUNISIA	ROMANIA	COLOMBIA

Monday June 22nd

MONTPELLIER (4.30PM)		TOULOUSE (8PM)	
COLOMBIA	TUNISIA	ROMANIA	ENGLAND

Friday June 26th

ST DENIS (8PM)		LENS (8PM)	
ROMANIA	TUNISIA	COLOMBIA	ENGLAND
WINNER		**RUNNER-UP**	

GROUP H

 ARGENTINA   JAPAN

 JAMAICA    CROATIA

Sunday June 14th

TOULOUSE (1.30PM)		LENS (8PM)	
ARGENTINA	JAPAN	JAMAICA	CROATIA

Saturday June 20th / Sunday June 21st

NANTES (1.30PM)		PARIS (2.30PM)	
JAPAN	CROATIA	ARGENTINA	JAMAICA

Friday June 26th

BORDEAUX (3PM)		LYON (3PM)	
ARGENTINA	CROATIA	JAPAN	JAMAICA
WINNER		**RUNNER-UP**	

FULL SPEED AHEAD FOR LA

SECOND ROUND

1. Saturday June 27th — Paris (8pm)
GROUP A WINNER V GROUP B RUNNER-UP

2. Saturday June 27th — Marseille (3.30pm)
GROUP B WINNER V GROUP A RUNNER-UP

3. Sunday June 28th — Lens (3.30pm)
GROUP C WINNER V GROUP D RUNNER-UP

4. Sunday June 28th — St Denis (8pm)
GROUP D WINNER V GROUP C RUNNER-UP

5. Monday June 29th — Toulouse (8pm)
GROUP E WINNER V GROUP F RUNNER-UP

6. Monday June 29th — Montpellier (3.30pm)
GROUP F WINNER V GROUP E RUNNER-UP

7. Tuesday June 30th — Bordeaux (3.30pm)
GROUP G WINNER V GROUP H RUNNER-UP

8. Tuesday June 30th — St Etienne (8pm)
GROUP H WINNER V GROUP G RUNNER-UP

QUARTER FINALS

1. Friday July 3rd — Nantes (8pm)
GAME 1 WINNER V GAME 4 WINNER

2. Friday July 3rd — St Denis (3.30pm)
GAME 2 WINNER V GAME 3 WINNER

3. Saturday July 4th — Marseille (3.30pm)
GAME 5 WINNER V GAME 8 WINNER

4. Saturday July 4th — Lyon (8pm)
GAME 6 WINNER V GAME 7 WINNER

GRANDE FINALE!

SEMI-FINALS

Tuesday July 7th   Marseille (8pm)

GAME 1 WINNER v GAME 3 WINNER

WORLD CUP FINAL

Sunday July 12th   St Denis (8pm)

SEMI-FINAL WINNERS

1998 WORLD CHAMPIONS

Wednesday July 8th   St Denis (8pm)

GAME 2 WINNER v GAME 4 WINNER

THIRD PLACE PLAY-OFF

Saturday July 11th   Paris (8pm)

SEMI-FINAL LOSERS

HERE'S WHERE IT HAPPENS

Nantes

STADE DE LA BEAUJOIRE

CAPACITY: 40,000

Montpellier

STADE DE LA MOSSON

CAPACITY: 35,500

Marseille

STADE VELODROME

CAPACITY: 60,000

Bordeaux

PARC LESCURE

CAPACITY: 36,500

Toulouse

STADIUM MUNICIPAL

CAPACITY: 37,000

Nantes

Bordeaux

Toulouse

St Etienne

STADE GEOFFROY-GUICHARD

CAPACITY: 36,000

Lyon

STADE DE GERLAND

CAPACITY: 44,000

Lens

STADE FELIX-BOLLAERT

CAPACITY: 42,000

St Denis

STADE DE FRANCE

CAPACITY: 80,000

Paris

PARC DES PRINCES

CAPACITY: 49,500

Lens

St Denis

Paris

Lyon

St Etienne

Montpellier

Marseille

ENGLAND'S LIKELY LADS

David Seaman
Arsenal

**PREVIOUS CLUBS: QPR,
BIRMINGHAM, PETERBOROUGH,
LEEDS UNITED**

HEIGHT: 6FT 4INS.

BORN: SEPTEMBER 19TH, 1963.

**FIRST CAP: SAUDI ARABIA 1
ENGLAND 1 (RIYADH) NOV 16TH,
1988.**

David Seaman is everything a good goalkeeper should be, commanding in the box, quick - thinking, brave and agile. He is without doubt England's No 1,

the foundation of the side and follows a proud tradition. England goalkeepers tend to collect more caps than there are hats at Ascot on Ladies' Day - Gordon Banks 73 caps, Ray Clemence 61 and Peter Shilton 125. Seaman was born in Rotherham in September 1963 and signed on as an apprentice with Leeds United in September 1981 but never played a first-team game for the Yorkshire club. Sold to Peterborough United for £4,000, he increased his value 25-fold after playing 91 League matches. Birmingham signed him for £100,000 in

October 1984 and he was to spend two seasons there before being bought for £225,000 by Queens Park Rangers. The move to Loftus Road raised his profile and, while there, he was capped by England for the first time. When Arsenal needed a new goalkeeper for the 1990-91 season, they bought Seaman for £1.3million. What a first season he had at Highbury! Arsenal won the title, lost just one match all season and conceded a miserly 18 goals in 38 matches. For England he has been a rock. The laid-back giant, revelling in his job, is an inspiration to his team-mates,

including those who are his rivals for the No 1 shirt. "I've been to many England games where David has not had a lot to do," says Nigel Martyn, "but he concentrates all the time, talks to his defenders and makes sure that when there are one or two things to do he is alert. Keeping your concentration is as much an art as pulling off eye-catching saves and while it is nice to do that, there can be no let-up. You have to watch all the time, staying on your toes, and David's record is proof that he is not one to be caught napping."

Nigel Martyn
Leeds United

PREVIOUS CLUBS: CRYSTAL PALACE, BRISTOL ROVERS.

HEIGHT: 6FT 2INS.

BORN AUGUST 11TH, 1966.

FIRST CAP: CIS 2 ENGLAND 2 (SUB)(MOSCOW) APRIL 29TH, 1992.

When George Graham took charge at Leeds United he did not know too much about Nigel Martyn, although as the man who signed David Seaman for Arsenal he knew a good goalkeeper when he saw one. It did not take Martyn long to impress the boss. "I hadn't realised how good he was," says Graham. "He's really surprised me. When, as I did at Arsenal, you have a goalkeeper like David Seaman, who I think is the best, you don't really appreciate the other 'keepers but he is very, very close to Seaman in ability." In the 1996-97 season Martyn was the king of the clean sheets with 19 as week

after week he produced breathtaking stops. Martyn, the first £1million goalkeeper in British football when he was signed from Bristol Rovers by Steve Coppell for Crystal Palace in November 1989, won three caps while at the south London club. He made his England debut as a substitute in April 1992, replacing Chris Woods in Moscow against the CIS, then started against Hungary two weeks later. A year later and he had the distinction of being the first England goalkeeper to play a full international indoors and on grass, when England played Germany in Detroit in the US Cup in 1993. Martyn says that the move to Leeds had been the tonic his game needed. That, along with the challenge of winning over a new set of fans, had made him better than when he first wore an England shirt. There has also been the small matter of his breaking the British transfer-fee record for a goalkeeper for a second time, when Leeds paid Palace £2.25million for his services.

Tim Flowers
Blackburn Rovers

PREVIOUS CLUBS: SOUTHAMPTON, WOLVERHAMPTON WANDERERS.

HEIGHT: 6FT 2INS.

BORN: FEBRUARY 3RD, 1967.

FIRST CAP: BRAZIL 1 ENGLAND 1 (WASHINGTON) JUNE 13TH, 1993.

Tim Flowers knows better than most that when it comes to gaffes, goalkeepers are in a league of their own. Nobody forgets them - not even when the man in the No 1 shirt is not to blame. Remember the Stan Collymore goal against Blackburn? A weak shot heading for the arms of Flowers hit a divot and took an unreal bounce over his shoulder. He was horrified and Collymore, then playing for Liverpool, looked highly embarrassed.Remember the breathtaking stops Flowers has

made? Well yes, but certainly not in such specific detail as the odd howler. Flowers has worked hard on his game and has earned England caps as understudy to David Seaman. But just when he seemed at the very least to be the automatic No 2 for as long as he wanted, he lost form. Since then he has climbed back into the ratings and is now involved in a pecking-order battle with Nigel Martyn, of Leeds.Ray Harford, his former manager at Blackburn, says: "He is very self-critical, but that's no bad thing. He's also very chirpy about most things. If Tim makes errors he accepts them, will work out in his own mind what went wrong and why - then he'll look forward."That positive attitude has brought Flowers back into the frame. The man whose name has given rise to a welter of horticultural punning headlines really is set to bloom for England.

Alan Shearer
Newcastle United

Previous clubs: Blackburn Rovers, Southampton.

Height: 5ft 11ins.

Born: August 13th 1970.

First cap: England 2 France 0 (scored) (Wembley) February 19th, 1992

Alan Shearer is the first man to score more than 30 goals in three consecutive seasons in the top flight since the 1930s and, but for an ankle injury, he would have been odds-on for another 30 in the 1997-98 season. In days of sky-high transfer fees Shearer, at a British record £15million, has proved to be value for money for Newcastle. He is the complete striker: strong, quick, brave and instinctive. Having him back from injury for France '98 will be a huge bonus and will lift an England squad already believing it can win the World Cup. Shearer started out as a trainee with Southampton, graduated to the first team and scored 23 goals in 118 games. Then Blackburn, just promoted to the Premiership, bought him at the start of the 1992-93 season for what was at the time a staggering £3.6million. It was money well spent. The striker everybody wanted, Shearer bowed to the sentimental pull of his roots to join Newcastle and insisted that he should wear the club's famous No 9 shirt. "He's a role model for all of us in the game - a fantastic footballer and off the pitch a really nice bloke, an inspiration to everyone," says David Beckham, England colleague but Manchester United rival. "He is a player that we all look up to, the man to give England a lead." It is a view echoed by Beckham's United team-mate Teddy Sheringham. "Alan is phenomenal," he says. "Defenders know all about him, will do whatever they can to stop him scoring - and he still manages to score goals regardless."

Sol Campbell
Tottenham

Previous clubs: None.

Height: 6ft 2ins.

Born: September 18th 1974.

First cap: England 3 Hungary 0 (sub)(Wembley) May 18th, 1996

Sol Campbell has taken to international football like a duck to water. Nothing intimidates him. Capped by England as a 21-year-old, Campbell has come through the ranks at Tottenham, where he has done more than establish himself in the first team. He has become the club's Mr Fixit, willing and able to play in defence, midfield or even as a makeshift striker. His strengths are his size and astonishing speed. Those two virtues would count for little were it nor for his superb reading of the game. How many times for England has Campbell appeared from nowhere to save a situation, daring to make full-impact tackles in his own penalty box and always pulling it off because of his measured timing and controlled body positioning? Born in Stratford, East London, he soon interested West Ham but at 14 and after three months at Upton Park, he left and Spurs were quick to pick him up. One of the successes of the FA School of Excellence at Lilleshall, Sol (christened Sulzeer) has played for England at youth, under-21 and B levels. He is still on the learning curve, getting better and better with every match. He recognises as much and so do Tottenham, who have improved his contract. For a man who once nearly gave it up to become an electrician, football life has just gone from good to better - and the best is yet to come. David Howells, Campbell's team-mate at Spurs, says: "Sol's main strength is his strength. He also has pace. He has come on incredibly and we talk about growing in stature but when he returned from the Tournoi de France he really did look bigger." Former Spurs manager Gerry Francis called him a dream player because of his willingness to work. "He's so adaptable and does well wherever he plays," says Francis. "He's so strong it's frightening."

Gareth Southgate
Aston Villa

PREVIOUS CLUB: CRYSTAL PALACE.

HEIGHT: 6FT.

BORN: SEPTEMBER 30TH 1970.

FIRST CAP: ENGLAND 1
PORTUGAL 1 (SUB)(WEMBLEY)
DECEMBER 12TH, 1995.

The chance to wipe away the memories of the penalty miss in Euro '96 cannot come quick enough for Southgate, who has found that awful moment overshadowing his otherwise considerable international achievements. His appearance in Euro '96 was evidence of what can be achieved by an ambitious player in a short space of time. Southgate had broken into the England squad only six months earlier. He worked up through the ranks at Crystal Palace and became captain. Then playing as a midfielder, he proved himself as articulate with a football at his feet as he was off the pitch dealing with the press but like all footballers, he wanted to win trophies and that was more likely at Aston Villa, who paid £2.5million for him in June 1995. Southgate, now a defender, played in the Villa team which won the 1996 Coca-Cola Cup, beating Leeds 3-0, and has become an increasingly influential member of the side, eventually being appointed captain at the start of the 1997-98 season. His strength is his ability to learn and respond to situations. He is a defender who likes to bring the ball out of defence rather than hoof it upfield and, if needs be, he will slot into the midfield again and play a battling game. Venables became a big fan and Glenn Hoddle, his successor, has

been equally impressed. But it was not always the case. When he joined Aston Villa, Paul McGrath was the man Southgate was due to replace. Says McGrath: "I was looking at him in training and I thought they were joking - he didn't even look like a centre half. I don't quite know what he looked like but he worked hard at his game and became the finest central defender I have played with."

Andy Hinchcliffe
Sheffield Wed

PREVIOUS CLUBS: EVERTON,
MANCHESTER CITY.

HEIGHT: 5FT 10INS.

BORN: FEBRUARY 5TH 1969.

FIRST CAP: MOLDOVA 0
ENGLAND 3 (CHISINAU)
SEPTEMBER 1ST, 1996.

There are easier games in which to make an international debut, but then Andy Hinchcliffe has always been able to cope with pressure, as he proved in the opening World Cup qualifying match in Group 2 in Moldova. An attacking left-back, he suffered a knee ligament injury which put him out of action for nine months and delayed his ultimate move to Sheffield Wednesday after earlier transfer talks with Spurs. Hinchcliffe is not your average footballer. For starters, he has more O-levels than fingers and an academic future seriously beckoned until Manchester City made him an offer. It was now or never and, realising he could return to studying later, Hinchcliffe decided to give it a go.

Paul Ince
Liverpool

PREVIOUS CLUBS: INTER MILAN,
MANCHESTER UNITED, WEST
HAM.

HEIGHT: 5FT 10INS.

BORN: OCTOBER 21ST 1967.

FIRST CAP: SPAIN 1 ENGLAND 0
(SANTANDER) SEPTEMBER 9TH,
1992.

Nicknamed "The Guv'nor" Paul Ince more than lived up to the image in Rome when England needed and got a draw with Italy to qualify automatically for France '98. That night he bossed the midfield and, even though his head was split open and he had to leave the pitch for repairs, he was soon back running the show, his shirt stained red with blood, his head bandaged. Ince is the sort of leader who doesn't expect people to do something he wouldn't do himself. Hard and combative, he can mix aggression with subtle skills. West Ham were his first club. He scored on his full debut against Southampton and became the darling of Upton Park until he joined Manchester United for £800,000 in 1989. There he settled into the midfield and was central to United's re-emergence as the powerhouse of English football. Ince became a key member of the England team, an automatic choice with Terry

Venables and then Glenn Hoddle. In June 1995, Ince moved from United to Inter Milan for £7.5million but his early days in Italy were a severe culture shock. It got better, but Ince made no attempt to hide the family unrest at being in Italy and returned home to Liverpool for £4.2million in July 1997 when Manchester United did not follow up their buy-back option from the original deal. Not that England have lost faith. Glenn Hoddle says: "The thing about Paul is that he knows he is an international player, he's got that inner assurance and has added to his talents by going abroad and taking the challenge. His main asset is that he is a winner."

After a successful outing for that first cap - a 3-0 win - Hinchcliffe was picked again for victories against Poland and Georgia, but then injury set him back and now he faces competition for the left wing-back position, Graeme Le Saux and Philip Neville all having a strong case. He has not let himself down. "He brings the quality of versatility to defence," says England team-mate Sol Campbell. "He has that air of assurance and is strong in the air and on the ground and really fits into the system well."

David Batty
Newcastle United

PREVIOUS CLUBS: BLACKBURN ROVERS, LEEDS.

HEIGHT: 5FT 8INS.

BORN: DECEMBER 2ND 1968.

FIRST CAP: ENGLAND 3 USSR 1 (SUB)(WEMBLEY) MAY 21ST, 1991.

David Batty is the Yorkshire-born terrier who came to prominence with his hometown club Leeds United and won a Championship medal with them, before moving on to make a big impact at Blackburn and Newcastle. Leeds fans took him to their hearts and Batty was a key figure in the club's successes of the 1991-92 season, when he slotted into a midfield that contained ball-playing maestros in Gary McAllister and Gordon Strachan, with Batty the bulldog in the middle. The balance was right but, the following season, the defence of the title foundered on a dismal away record. Batty, however, was still the key man at Leeds when Kenny Dalglish signed him for Blackburn in 1993 for £2.5million. In his first season he was the club's player of the year. His influence at Blackburn, however, was restricted by an ankle injury which resulted in his impact on the club's Premiership title win being limited to a

handful of appearances. But when he was fit again Newcastle, at the time managed by Kevin Keegan, moved in with a £3.75million offer. Batty has again become the heart of the side around which everything revolves but, despite his endeavour and the occasional valuable goal, Newcastle struggled to string together the sort of results expected from a club with their resources. Even so they got value for money. As Keegan says: "He was outstanding, better than we ever thought he was - an exceptional player. Critics say he can't pass the ball but they are wrong. He is in fact an outstanding passer."

Graeme Le Saux
Chelsea

PREVIOUS CLUBS: BLACKBURN ROVERS, CHELSEA.

HEIGHT: 5FT 10INS.

BORN: OCTOBER 17TH 1968.

FIRST CAP: ENGLAND 1 DENMARK 0 (SUB)(WEMBLEY) MARCH 9TH, 1994.

The first player from the Channel Isles to be capped - he beat Matt Le Tissier to that honour by minutes when selected to start against Denmark, while Le Tissier was a substitute called on later - Le Saux is an attacking full-back who has rediscovered his zest for the game. He is one of the game's more intriguing characters because he does not conform to the stereotypical image of a footballer. He prefers to read The Guardian and in his free time to visit museums and art galleries. Le Saux was discovered by Chelsea playing for St Paul's in Jersey and made his top-flight debut on Boxing Day 1989. Switched between midfield and defence and caught in the crossfire of managerial changes, Le Saux realised he was going stale, his game suffered and eventually he was sold to Blackburn Rovers for £750,000. At Ewood Park, he reverted to defence and helped Rovers to win the Premiership title. Injury wrecked most of his 1995-96 season and when manager Kenny Dalglish left Blackburn, Le Saux fell out with Tony Parkes, the assistant manager, and asked for a transfer. Blackburn priced him at £7.5million but finally accepted an offer of £5million from Chelsea, the club who had sold him and now admitted that it had been a mistake. Chelsea manager

at that time, Ruud Gullit agreed he was putting right a wrong. He said: "Graeme is an international who has already shown people what he is capable of. He has experience and it is difficult to buy that cheaply."

Nicky Butt
Man United

PREVIOUS CLUBS: NONE.

HEIGHT: 6FT.

BORN: JUNE 25TH, 1973.

FIRST CAP: ENGLAND 2, MEXICO 0 (SUB)(WEMBLEY) MARCH 29TH, 1997.

There was a hole in the Manchester United midfield made by the departure of Paul Ince and a long-term injury to Roy Keane. Most managers would have reached for the cheque-book, but most managers don't have a Nicky Butt coming through the ranks. Butt has grabbed his chance with such aplomb that he has rocketed from the already considerable height of holding down a place with United to become an international star in the making. His first two England games were as a substitute and he immediately showed he was not going to be overawed. "Nicky reminds me a bit of myself at that age," says Ince. "I had that same never-say-die attitude. He's got massive heart and determination. He probably gets forward a bit more than I do and I think he has the potential to be one of the best players in Europe." Nurtured through the United youth system,

Butt made his debut as a substitute in 1992 in a 3-2 win over Oldham and has got better and better. A fearless player with a hardened edge and tidy skills, he is a crucial component in the United team. He was capped at youth, schools and under-21 level by England, and though the down side is that he does suffer from the odd red-mist moment, he knows that both Alex Ferguson and Glenn Hoddle will not tolerate any high-profile bad behaviour and the responsibility to shape up is his alone. A golden future beckons and England certainly need his skills, his courage, his heart and aggression directed in a positive way.

Teddy Sheringham
Man United

PREVIOUS CLUBS: TOTTENHAM, NOTTINGHAM FOREST, MILLWALL.

HEIGHT: 6FT.

BORN: APRIL 2ND 1966.

FIRST CAP: POLAND 1 ENGLAND 1 (CHORZOW) MAY 29TH, 1993.

Alan Shearer may score the lion's share of the goals but he needs someone to feed him, and in Teddy Sheringham he has the perfect foil. The two go together like salt and pepper. Sheringham, however, has done better than that. With Shearer out injured for a large part of the English 1997-98 domestic season, Sheringham, admired by Glenn Hoddle, has risen to the challenge of filling the void and has done it with success. He started out as an apprentice with Millwall making his first appearance in the 1983-84 season, and scored one goal in seven matches. It was a time when the south London side were on the up and Sheringham

formed a mighty partnership with Tony Cascarino, the Republic of Ireland striker. Both men scored goals galore as Millwall topped the Second Division in 1988 and went on to enjoy one good season in the top flight, the club's first appearance at that level,

before being relegated in 1989-90. Then Nottingham Forest, in desperate need of a goalscorer, paid £2million for him and in one full season at the City Ground, Sheringham scored at the rate of a goal every three games. Home-sickness set in and after just three

matches for Forest in his second season, he was off again - back to London and to Tottenham. Forest made a small profit, selling him for £2.1million. Good strikers will always score goals, irrespective of the company they are keeping, and Sheringham passed this test with flying colours. In 38 games in his first season with Spurs he scored 21 goals and formed solid partnerships with Jurgen Klinsmann and Chris Armstrong. Then when Eric Cantona left Manchester United in the summer of 1997, it became clear that Alex Ferguson would want a tried-and-trusted replacement. Sheringham, at £3.5million, was the man and he has more than lived up to expectations. His England colleague Ian Wright says: "I've always liked Teddy because he thrives on the same hunger and desire for goals as me. Watch him and you'll see he rarely has a bad game - even when he doesn't score.He is a good team player and the ideal partner. I just wish I'd played more games alongside him at international level."

Tony Adams
Arsenal

PREVIOUS CLUBS: NONE.

HEIGHT: 6FT 3INS.

BORN: OCTOBER 10TH 1966.

FIRST CAP: SPAIN 2 ENGLAND 4 (MADRID) FEB 18TH, 1987.

Tony Adams is the model professional of his era, which says a lot about his resolve and attitude considering the problems he has had down the years. He's been labelled a donkey, was dropped from the England 1990 World Cup squad, was jailed after being convicted for drink-driving, fell down the stairs of a night-club and ended up needing 29 stitches in a cut above his eye, dropped a team-mate in a League Cup celebration and broke his arm and finally, in September 1996, admitted he was an

alcoholic. Yet today Tony Adams is a happier man, content and able to cope with the pressures of top-class professional football and is keen to make the most of it, as international team-mate Paul Ince acknowledges. "For guys like myself and Tony Adams, this is our last chance," says Ince. "We had one against Germany in Euro '96 and missed it so we are lucky to have another opportunity and for players like myself and Tony, we are determined to make the most of it. We're better equipped, stronger and better - we want to win." A one-club man, Adams made his Arsenal debut back in the 1983-84 season and has been the beacon of the club's defence. He was one of the main reasons why in the 1990-91 season, when Arsenal won the championship, they conceded a staggeringly low 18 goals in 38 matches. Yet there is more to Adams than leading a

back-line that is rigidly disciplined and technically skilled. Adams is a defender who can score goals and he is always a threat in dead-ball situations. The trials and tribulations of the years, he says, have made him a better person and opened up worlds that earlier he would never have dreamed

existed. He has taken up the piano, is studying English literature and now leaves training to go to the opera or visit an art gallery. Adams might not be the fastest defender but with quick men around him to mop up, he can construct as good a stone wall as to be found anywhere.

Rio Ferdinand
West Ham

PREVIOUS CLUBS: NONE.

HEIGHT: 6FT 2INS.

BORN: NOVEMBER 7TH 1978.

FIRST CAP: ENGLAND 2, CAMEROON 0 (SUB)(WEMBLEY) NOVEMBER 15TH, 1997

Even in the fast world of football, Ferdinand's rise has been electric. Now it is amazing to look back and see that, until the 1997-98 season, he was yet to be a regular in the Premiership. Even so, he had made a huge impression in a few games. Ferdinand's route to the top has been boosted by Glenn Hoddle's willingness to encourage talented youngsters by inviting them to England training sessions so that they can have an early taste of life as an international. The first time that happened, during Euro 96, Ferdinand - cousin of Tottenham and England striker Les - had completed just one full match for West Ham. When the letter arrived with the three-lions stamp, Ferdinand read it and thought there had to be some mistake. Ferdinand is a happy mix of self-confidence and naivety and has a healthy respect for the past. He regrets that he never saw Bobby Moore play for West Ham, takes on board with pride that he has been compared with England's World Cup-winning captain and then disarmingly admits that some of his mates he used to play Sunday football with are better players than he is. There is no doubt that he is a player born into the job. His skill is such that, though a relative Premier League novice, he has the cool to handle the tense situations and refuses to be intimidated by the physical stuff. Even so, his full international career was delayed after he was dropped from the England squad following a drink-drive conviction. John Hartson, his West Ham colleague and a Wales international, says: "Rio's punishment was a painful one - to be left out of the England squad on the eve of his international debut - but he is a level-headed lad and the lesson will have been learned. The way a player can face up to adversity has a lot to do with overcoming the problem and I have no worries that Rio will go on to become a major part of England's future."

David Beckham
Man United

PREVIOUS CLUBS: NONE.

HEIGHT: 6FT.

BORN: MAY 2ND 1975.

FIRST CAP: MOLDOVA 0 ENGLAND 3 (CHISINAU) SEPTEMBER 1ST, 1996.

The future of English football is David Beckham. The Manchester United youngster has not just arrived on the scene as a star, he has exploded on it. Goals are the name of the game and when Beckham gets them, he gets them in style. He has gone from strength to strength with United and earned his call-up to the England team for the first of the World Cup qualifying matches, against Moldova, in 1996. Beckham was brought up in Essex, where his parents and two sisters still live. The turning point, however, came when as an 11-year-old he won a football skills competition organised by Bobby Charlton. The United legend gave him a piece of advice that Beckham has followed to the letter: "Shoot at all times if you've got the chance." He played for Essex Boys, trained with Tottenham Hotspur - where he insisted on wearing his Manchester United shirt - and had trials at West Ham, but he went north to join United's training scheme, stayed in digs and saw his family down south only at weekends. His first significant contribution for the Old Trafford club came when as a 20-year-old, he scored the winner against Chelsea in the 1996 FA Cup semi-final. It was a big goal on a big stage, but Beckham has not been overawed by the success or the endless headlines about his fiancée, Spice Girl Victoria - the posh one. "David has a lot going for him," says former team-mate Paul Ince. "He has plenty of talent and will be a strong midfielder for years to come. His future is very exciting. His passing is his talent, his maturity is to do with staying calm on the ball when he needs to. He makes decisions and selections on the pitch in a cool way, far more advanced than his age suggests."

Martin Keown
Arsenal

PREVIOUS CLUBS: EVERTON, ASTON VILLA, ARSENAL.

HEIGHT: 6FT 1INS.

BORN: JULY 24TH, 1966.

FIRST CAP: ENGLAND 2 FRANCE 0 (WEMBLEY) FEBRUARY 19TH, 1992.

Martin Keown is almost one of the forgotten men of football. Never really the target for a mega-money move but going for a tidy sum on several occasions, he has always seemed to be on the periphery of the first team at club and international level.Perhaps it is a case of seen and not heard for within the game Keown is rated - and though in his thirties now, he is getting better. A tough, uncompromising defender who built up a reputation as a limpet-like man-marker, Keown has refined his skills so that today, when he wins the ball, he no longer hoofs it into row Z of the stand. He joined Arsenal as an apprentice and, in between two spells on loan at Brighton, appeared in 22 matches for the Gunners. Then a contract dispute saw him move to Aston Villa. Next it was Everton, before he returned to Highbury in a £2million deal in the 1992-93 season. Adaptable, Keown won his first caps in 1992 and marked his second game in an England shirt with a rare but scorching goal in a 2-2 draw with Czechoslovakia in Prague. But after 11 internationals he faded from sight. Then, after four years and following two very good seasons at Arsenal, he was back for England to face Mexico. "I never gave up hope of coming back but the longer it goes, the more you wonder."

Paul Scholes
Man United

PREVIOUS CLUBS: NONE.

HEIGHT: 5FT 7INS.

BORN: NOVEMBER 16TH, 1974.

FIRST CAP: ENGLAND 2 SOUTH AFRICA 1 (SUB)(OLD TRAFFORD) MAY 24TH, 1997.

Paul Scholes made his third England start the day before his 23rd birthday and celebrated with a spectacular goal against Cameroon that had Glenn Hoddle describing him as a jewel in the nation's footballing crown.
The asthma-suffering Scholes has come a long way in a short time. He has rid himself of a reputation for being a hot-head and instead has been compared by his United manager, Alex Ferguson, to Kenny Dalglish in his playing pomp. At Old Trafford, Scholes has settled effortlessly into a side suddenly and unexpectedly shorn of one of its major stars, Eric Cantona. Yet Scholes has eased the pain. Where Cantona was the strutting master of all he surveyed, Scholes is the sniping destroyer. In the process he has won over the old heads. "His vision is superb and his touch and awareness fantastic," says team-mate Gary Pallister. "There is very much an element of Eric in him. He is a very crafty and intelligent young player. Paul always takes a little look over his shoulder before he decides what to do - he knows all the time what is happening." Scholes is an all-action player always wanting the ball, forever urging on his team. He is a potent substitute able to come into the thick of the action, pick up the tempo and dictate the shape of the rest of the game. There have been valuable goals all down the line, whatever the company. Much of United's European Championship League success was founded on touches of Scholes' magic. Even those outside United have taken to him, as was proved from his performance against Cameroon. The Wembley crowd had been singing "Stand up if you hate Man United," but the moment Scholes passed them as Chris Sutton replaced him with ten minutes left, they burst into spontaneous applause.

Philip Neville
Man United

PREVIOUS CLUBS: NONE.

HEIGHT: 5FT 10INS.

BORN: JANUARY 21ST, 1977.

FIRST CAP: CHINA 0 ENGLAND 3 (BEIJING) MAY 23RD, 1996.

The Neville brothers, Philip and Gary, are the first to have played in the same England team since Bobby and Jack Charlton and both look natural internationals. Philip in fact is the younger and was the first to show for England when picked to face China back in 1996. The Neville brothers have built up quite a reputation as a double-act. When with England they room together and some swear that, when one of them is injured, the other though fully fit has also struggled. Yet Philip might easily have played professional cricket - he has England cricket caps at under-14 and under-15 age groups. It was only the lure of Manchester United which distracted him. Philip's rise since then has been spectacular. He had played only twice for United prior to the start

of the 1995-96 season, but his strength in the air allied to tough tackling won him the United right-back spot from brother Gary. "Philip is too good," said brother Gary. "He looks more comfortable on the ball than me and one of his main strengths is going forward." Phil admits that United's policy of playing youngsters, if they are good enough, has helped his career and says that the atmosphere at the club, where the seasoned professionals are willing to help and encourage the juniors, has played a big part in his success.

Steve McManaman
Liverpool

PREVIOUS CLUBS: NONE.

HEIGHT: 6FT.

BORN: FEBRUARY 11TH, 1972.

FIRST CAP: ENGLAND 1 NIGERIA 0 (SUB)(WEMBLEY) NOVEMBER 16TH, 1994

On his day, Steve McManaman is a world-beater capable of running the length of the pitch with the ball at his feet and finishing with a stunning shot. There are the other times when he does a Harry Houdini and disappears from sight, even though he's there all the time. McManaman has proved he is a big-match man and his role there, as a roving midfielder, suits him fine. But he knows that he has to be responsible and get back to help out the defence. He also knows he needs to be a more regular goalscorer. "He's such a brilliant big-game player," says colleague Jamie Redknapp. "When he's most under pressure he will perform to his best. It's the sort of temperament you need at international level. Macca's a genuine down-to-earth lad but dead smart. So intelligent that he never gets the mickey taken out of him by the other players - he's too sharp, they leave him alone." For England, his strength is the space he makes with his runs and Glenn Hoddle wants him to add to his game, to hone a sharper edge in the last third of the field and provide for the forwards. Hoddle believes if he does that, then the goals will come. An Everton fan who was picked up by Liverpool, McManaman came through the ranks at Anfield and won England youth and under-21 caps before becoming the target and subject of much European transfer speculation. Off field, McManaman cultivates the image of the thinking footballer - so successfully that he has had a column in The Times.

Gary Neville
Man United

PREVIOUS CLUBS: NONE.

HEIGHT: 5FT 10INS.

BORN: FEBRUARY 18TH, 1975.

FIRST CAP: ENGLAND 2 JAPAN 1 (WEMBLEY) JUNE 3RD, 1995.

Ousted from the full-back position at Manchester United by his brother Philip, Gary Neville has gone on to make a virtue of that inconvenience to become a genuine utility player, as accomplished on the right flank as he is switching to the middle of defence. A hard-tackling player who is quick, he is two years older than brother Philip. Gary was the first to come through at Old Trafford and the first to make it to the full England team, but these are brothers determined to help each other out and not scoring meaningless points off one another. That attitude was evident after Gary was booked in Euro '96 and, because of that, was forced to watch the semi-final against Germany. Angry with himself but accepting he was at fault, he then showed that his main concern was not his own misery but about England winning through to the final. The Alex Ferguson philosophy to give youth a chance has certainly been readily embraced by Gary but then, he is a clean-cut young man drawing considerable strength from the family unit - so much so that even though he recently bought his own house, more often than not he will be back at the family semi, enjoying his mother's cooking and chatting with the rest of the family. Brother Phil says: "If I had some of Gary's attributes I'd be a much better player than I am now. He's a good defender, he heads the ball well and reads the game brilliantly. He's been the United youth team captain and leads by example, so I'm always learning from him."

Ian Wright
Arsenal

PREVIOUS CLUB: CRYSTAL PALACE.

HEIGHT: 5FT 9INS.

BORN: NOVEMBER 3RD 1963.

FIRST CAP: ENGLAND 2 CAMEROON 0 (WEMBLEY) FEBRUARY 6TH, 1991

Better late than never for Ian Wright, one of the late starters in the professional game. He made his debut in his early twenties for Crystal Palace first team, but has lived every minute for all it is worth. A hero at Palace, a god at Arsenal, Wright is one of football's real characters with a natural goalscoring instinct and a nose for controversy. Having helped Palace to the top flight and an FA Cup final - where he scored twice - Wright was then signed by George Graham for Arsenal for £2.5million in September 1991. He has gone on to break Cliff Bastin's club scoring record. He has found the international stage less accommodating and it took nine games for him to score his first goal for England - a key World Cup qualifying match with Poland in 1993. His international career then went on hold and he was left out of the side throughout 1996 until Glenn Hoddle reinstated him. Wright took his chance in style. He was a star in England's Tournoi de France win in 1997, scoring a memorable goal against Italy and then setting one up for Paul Scholes to show that, even though he is in his mid-thirties, there is still plenty of life in him. What's more, he is rated by his fellow professionals. Dennis Bergkamp, the Dutch

striker and Arsenal team-mate, says: "Ian is the best finisher I have ever seen. Other strikers have different styles, but if you look purely at goalscoring and the way Ian touches the ball that makes a goal for someone else, he is in a league of his own." Alan Shearer is not slow to agree with Bergkamp's assessment of Wright. "He's a great athlete and has tremendous enthusiasm," says Shearer. "You only have to look at his Arsenal goalscoring record to see how good he is. Give him half a second and it's probably too much - as many defenders know to their cost."

Michael Owen
Liverpool

PREVIOUS CLUBS: NONE.

HEIGHT: 5FT 8INS.

BORN: DECEMBER 14TH 1979.

FIRST CAP: ENGLAND 0 CHILE 2 (WEMBLEY) FEBRUARY 11TH, 1998

The wonder boy of the 1997-98 season, Michael Owen had been touted as something special from the moment he broke Ian Rush's scoring record for Deeside School, hitting 97 in a 42-match season - 25 more than the Liverpool legend managed in his time. From then on, Liverpool were determined to sign this son of a former Everton player and the world was not far behind with Arsenal and Manchester United both more than a little interested. By the time he was 15 Owen had signed his first kit deal and, at 17, Liverpool gave him a five-year contract worth £2.5million. Hot property indeed! Owen has a reputation and has lived up to it on the pitch. "He's a gem," says Steve Heighway, the Anfield

youth development officer. "He's very popular with the other lads and he is very strong mentally as well as being technically gifted. I've no doubts about him - he just needs to carry on as he has been." Playing for Liverpool meant finding a place in a side that has Robbie Fowler and Karl Heinz-Reidle in the forward line, but that was no problem. Handed a first-team squad shirt, No 18, he has fitted in with style and climbed into the top eleven. He made his debut towards the end of the 1996-97 season and became Liverpool's second youngest first-team player. He marked that occasion, against Wimbledon, with a goal after 17 minutes of first-team action and has made a habit of scoring ever since. His strengths are his pace and speed of reaction. On top of that he is a two-footed player and despite being small, he will not be intimidated. His knack of finding space and timing runs would make an old pro envious. Owen has been capped by England at under-16, 18, 20 and 21 levels. He skippered the under-18 side but suffered the one black moment of his career when he was sent off in a draw with Yugoslavia. Owen, however, has the impudence of youth, has proved himself an instant hit and could be the surprise package in Hoddle's final plans. The evidence has thus far been first-class.

Robert Lee
Newcastle United

PREVIOUS CLUB: CHARLTON ATHLETIC.

HEIGHT: 5FT 10INS.

BORN: FEBRUARY 1ST 1966.

FIRST CAP: ENGLAND 1 ROMANIA 1 (SCORED)(WEMBLEY) OCTOBER 12TH, 1994.

One of those players who receives a bigger fanfare from his fellow professionals than he does from spectators, Robert Lee has been in and around the England squad since 1994 but has yet to pass the 20-cap mark. That is partly down to injury. But if a job needs doing, Lee is the man. Born within a stone's throw of West Ham, the east London club was the one he wanted to join. Ironically, he was to play for a Charlton side managed by Alan Curbishley, who had been a player at West Ham when Lee first arrived on the scene. Curbishley could see Lee was the real thing. "He was in a schoolboy training group I used to take twice a week and I rated him highly then," says Curbishley. "I always thought he was good enough to play for England." Signed as a 16-year-old by Charlton, Lee served the club for nine seasons, operating as a centre forward or a winger. "We'd been telling people for years how good Robert was but we genuinely didn't get any offers for him until just before Newcastle made their move," adds Curbishley. West Ham and Middlesbrough were in the bidding, Newcastle won and Lee went north to become a cult figure at St James' Park. Terry Venables was the first to call him up for England and those years of slotting in at Charlton immediately paid dividends. Lee is the ideal standby man, the player to come in for someone who is injured and he will not disappoint. In fact, but for the gap between internationals, he might well have had enough matches under his belt to pin down a permanent place. The engine-room and the driving force at Newcastle, Lee is a players' player who has always been top-class even if it has taken the watching public a little longer to appreciate his talents.

Andy Cole
Man United

PREVIOUS CLUBS: NEWCASTLE UNITED, BRISTOL CITY, ARSENAL.

HEIGHT: 5FT 11INS.

BORN: OCTOBER 15TH 1971.

FIRST CAP: ENGLAND 0 URUGUAY 0 (SUB)(WEMBLEY) MARCH 29TH, 1995.

Sold by Arsenal for what is now a cut-price £500,000 to Bristol City, Cole became hot property in the West Country with 12 goals in 29 games and Newcastle United, then in the First Division, moved sharply to sign him for £1.75million. From that point on he just could not stop scoring goals. There were a remarkable 34 from 40 League matches in the 1993-94 promotion season as Cole fired Newcastle's Premiership campaign. But after nine goals in 18 games, Kevin Keegan sensationally sold him to arch-rivals Manchester United for £7million in January 1995. At Old Trafford life was not so easy but Alex Ferguson knows that a prolific goalscorer does not become bad overnight and with careful support, Cole returned to red-hot form. He became deadly again around the six-yard box, his reading of the game grew match-by-match, and he has made an invaluable contribution to the United cause. Cole's international experience may be limited but he is without doubt one of the form strikers in the English game. He has shown he can cope with pressure, that he can work on his game and that he won't let a bad run get him down. "He's been up among the top-scoring Premiership strikers and deservedly so," says rival Ian Wright. "Andy is one of the best in the business at making an opening with a quick turn. He's proved he can score goals at the highest level with both Newcastle and Manchester United and, come the start of every season, you know he's going to take some beating. He has persevered at Manchester United and it has all come good - not that he ever thought it wouldn't."

Paul Gascoigne
Rangers

PREVIOUS CLUBS: LAZIO, TOTTENHAM, NEWCASTLE.

HEIGHT: 5FT 10INS

BORN: MAY 27TH 1967.

FIRST CAP: ENGLAND 1 DENMARK 0 (SUB) (WEMBLEY) SEPTEMBER 14TH, 1988.

The joker who can't keep out of the spotlight, Paul Gascoigne has spent much of his career fighting a self-destructive urge that has been redeemed by moments of footballing genius. He was adored at Newcastle United, where he played 106 times and scored 22 goals, before joining Tottenham in 1988 for £2million. In an eventful fortnight, he made his debut with the London club at St James' Park in a 2-2 draw, then 11 days later won his first full England cap. Gascoigne's hour came in the World Cup in Italy in 1990 when he became an immediately recognisable global star after wearing his heart on his sleeve, as England reached the semi-finals. There were tears when Gascoigne was booked during the match, which meant that had England won, he would have been forced to miss the final. At Tottenham he won an FA Cup winners' medal in the 1991 final, even though he damaged cruciate knee ligaments in the opening minutes and was carried off and out of football for 16 months. Three knee operations later, Gascoigne was fit and ready to play - this time in Italy for Lazio who had paid £5.5million for his services. Rangers brought him back to Britain at the start of the 1995-96 season and he became a key figure in helping the Glasgow side to an eighth consecutive Scottish League title. With that success came the rejuvenation of his international career and he was to spearhead England's march to the semi-finals of Euro '96, his finest hour-and-a-half coming in the 4-1 thrashing of

Holland in the group stage. On that Wembley night Gascoigne was sensational, full of running and deft touches. "I enjoy playing alongside Gazza," says Paul Ince.

Jamie Redknapp
Liverpool

PREVIOUS CLUB: BOURNEMOUTH.

HEIGHT: 6FT.

BORN: JUNE 25TH, 1973.

FIRST CAP: ENGLAND 0 COLOMBIA 0 (WEMBLEY) SEPTEMBER 6TH, 1995

The son of West Ham manager Harry Redknapp, Jamie signed as a schoolboy for Tottenham Hotspur but made his professional debut at Bournemouth and was quickly the talk of the town. Liverpool, then managed by Kenny Dalglish, paid £350,000 in 1990 to buy the 17-year-old from Bournemouth. At Anfield he quickly earned a reputation as a fine passer of the ball. That is a quality not lost on Glenn Hoddle who sees Redknapp as a sweeper because of his ability to hit long, searching passes. Opportunities, however, have been restricted by injury. He might have been out of sight but certainly not out of

"I'm happy to be in front of the defence so I can pick and choose when to go forward and allow Gazza room to make things happen. I'm there to organise

mind and he has been invited to train with England even when not in serious contention for a place. The Liverpool team of the 1990s, while filled with supremely gifted footballers, has not lived up to the deeds of former Anfield sides and Redknapp has often been in the firing line when the guns of criticism have been discharged. However, the accusation that he doesn't care enough about the

everything. That gives us a chance to stamp our authority on the game and I feel we complement each other pretty well."

team is wide of the mark. Redknapp can often be found at the training ground on his days off, when he will be working hard in the company of Steve McManaman, Robbie Fowler and Jason McAteer. He knows that talent and self-confidence are not enough. When Terry Venables, as former England coach, lumped Redknapp and David Beckham together as the future of England, he was stating a real position rather than airing a hope. Venables was not the only one to do that. When Redknapp replaced the injured David Platt for England in October 1995, Platt said: "He is an outstanding talent and I have no doubts that one day he will captain his country." But it is Harry Redknapp, the West Ham manager, who knows his son best: "Jamie was totally dedicated and fortunately he has the ability. He was barely seven when I realised he had a football brain. He understands the game and how to be part of a team."

THE BACKROOM TEAM

Napoleon had a point when he said:

"An army marches on its stomach."

Every campaign, be it a fly-in, fly-out World Cup qualifier in Moldova or a four-week plus march through the World Cup finals in France, needs intensive backroom planning - the food to keep the army fighting, the Ralgex spray and TLC to keep a football team on its mettle.

England can expect a lot, but wouldn't get much without the expertise of the back-up team assembled by Glenn Hoddle, men and women appointed not just to do a job with quiet efficiency but also to mould into a cohesive unit and create the right atmosphere with the players.

A happy team is a winning team, and that will never change.

Hoddle has surrounded himself with trusty lieutenants on the coaching front, men who understand his philosophy, can see the pattern that he wants to cut, can help achieve that and offer a sounding board for ideas. But not only do they worry about the England playing staff, they will analyse the opponents and devise strategies for blunting the attacking edge of rivals.

There is a Tottenham circa early-1980s look to the present England set-up. Hoddle has as his No 2 John Gorman, a former team-mate at Tottenham and also his assistant at Swindon Town.

Also helping out are Glenn Roeder and Peter Taylor, while the specialist area of goalkeeping is in the safe hands of Ray Clemence. These men, under Hoddle's guidance, will direct the playing show but all their efforts would be meaningless without the rest of the supporting cast.

Next up is the medical team, a group of men who know that they will have work to do, and often in a very pressurised

environment. The England team doctor is Dr John Crane, who also handles the diet requirements of the squad. He is backed up by two physiotherapists - Gary Lewin, who does the job at Arsenal, and Alan Smith - while Steve Slattery is the squad masseur, who literally has his hands full when it comes to dealing with aches and pains.

Intelligence is vital, the low-down on opponents and the chance to review what has happened with his own training sessions, and Hoddle will more than likely be spending considerable time with Gary Guyar, the man responsible for videoing England's training sessions.

Guyar will tape, edit and produce the film evidence to back up hunches and feelings that the coaches bring to the table after a training session. His camera will mean that there is no place to hide; players motivated by the sheer magnitude of the occasion and the knowledge that for most of them it is a once-in-a-lifetime experience, will have little chance to disguise knocks and strains that might keep them out of the playing equation.

Keeping this lot in order and the team equipped also requires a professional approach and that means plenty of work for Martin Grogan, the England kit man, and for Michelle Farrer, who will handle the paperwork. "There is no limit to the size of the back-up team you take," says Steve Double, the FA spokesman. "It is a case of putting together the staff you need to do the job."

Hoddle, through his vast experience as player and now manager, knows only too well how important the crew will be and that team bonding is crucial.

When England played Cameroon at

Wembley in November 1997, the team were staying at their usual haunt, Bisham Abbey. But the night before the match, Hoddle block-booked an Italian restaurant and took the team and staff out for the night - away from the prying eyes of reporters and the probing of camera lenses.

"It was my way of saying well done," he said. "My thanks to the lads, the team

and the backroom staff for getting us to France. We didn't really have a chance after Rome but I think it helped towards the sense of togetherness and the team spirit."

Significantly, Hoddle made sure to include players involved in the whole of the qualifying campaign and not just those in the squad for the draw in Rome that secured a place in the World Cup,

and those due to face Cameroon. All the skill in the world will not be enough in France; temperament and support from all within the squad is essential. "There will be occasions when boredom sets in, that's inevitable," added Hoddle. "But I have to consider in my final equation those who are better suited to being away from home for five or six weeks."

No stone can be left unturned in the quest for glory and if it is achieved, no contribution will be less than any other. The England backroom team might not be seen at work by the public but there are some long hours still to be worked. Everybody counts, through to goal-getter Alan Shearer and the man who runs the players' bath at Wembley.

OUR NEXT TARGET

By Alec McGivan,
Campaign Director - England 2006

The heritage of England as the birthplace of the modern game is unrivalled in world football. It is the home of world-famous clubs such as Manchester United, Liverpool and Arsenal, whose grounds are shrines to fans across the globe. But it is not simply the powerful sense of history that makes English football so appealing - it is a game with a truly cosmopolitan flavour. England is now the favourite destination of fans and players from around the world. Every season, thousands make the pilgrimage to watch English teams studded with international stars playing skilful and exciting football. Foreign interest in English football is now at an all-time high. There are, currently, more than 140 overseas players representing nearly 40 different countries playing in the FA Premier League alone. Premier League action is broadcast to 122 nations and the FA Cup Final attracts a world-wide audience of 400 million. The modern English game is played in stadiums that are state-of-the-art and purpose-built for football. Over £600million has already been spent on a modernisation programme which has transformed England's leading venues into all-seater stadiums. English grounds epitomise the FIFA ideal: there are no ugly fences, no running tracks to separate the crowd from the pitch and no intrusive policing. Our stadiums are now places for families to enjoy, a fact that is borne out by the increasing numbers of women, children and disabled people who regularly attend matches. It is no wonder that attendances at League games have risen in ten of the eleven seasons since 1986. In short, English football is thriving, and it is on this basis that we are campaigning to bring the World Cup back to these shores forty years after we first staged the tournament. Our campaign to host the World Cup in 2006 reflects the unique

© 1997 F.A. TM

combination of tradition and innovation which England offers. There will, undoubtedly, be strong competition for football's greatest prize, but we believe that we have the best case. We are conducting a positive campaign which reflects the passion of the English game and the professionalism with which it is run. Nothing illustrates England's case more forcefully than Euro 96. By common consent, this tournament was the most successful European Championship ever - a sporting festival which established England's credentials as a host for major modern-day sporting events. The three- week tournament attracted almost 1.3 million spectators and a record television audience of 6.68 billion viewers from 192 countries. Perhaps even more significant was the fact that this was a trouble-free tournament, achieved through a policy of low-profile policing and high-profile stewarding. Another exciting feature of England's bid is the plan to redevelop Wembley Stadium. The Venue of Legends is to be transformed at a cost of over £200million and will be the centrepiece of a World Cup held in England. The famous Twin Towers will remain but the rest of the stadium will be remodelled in a futuristic yet sensitive fashion. This will ensure that Wembley continues to be the venue where every fan wants to watch football and where every footballer dreams of playing. Looking forward to 2006, the Football Association is confident that we can stage the best World Cup tournament ever; building on the success of Euro 96, buoyed by the thriving domestic game and eagerly awaiting the new Wembley Stadium. We can offer the best facilities, superb organisation and a friendly atmosphere.
We are ready to welcome the world.

GOLIATH 17 DAVID 0

by Chris Dighton

Yesterday's giants, tomorrow's Davids, but if Iran reach the World Cup Final they will have played 24 matches in their quest for football's ultimate prize. The journey started in appropriate surroundings, on the road to Damascus, the place the miniscule Maldive Islands had made home for their World Cup campaign. On a June afternoon in 1997, Iran smashed their hosts 17-0 for a record qualifying win.

The Maldive Islands, one of the 170 countries taking part in the 1998 competition, were beaten on all fronts, out-played, out-resourced and critically out-weighed. They took to the field with a goalkeeper who was only five foot seven inches, the rest of the squad averaged a good four to five inches shorter than their opponents and two stones lighter - literally a David and Goliath contest.

Five more games later, 59 goals conceded and none scored, FIFA insisted that the series had been an important learning experience for The Maldives. For the record, they lost 12-0 home and away to Syria, 9-0 in the return with Iran, 6-0 at home to Kyrgyzstan and, almost something to celebrate, a commendable 3-0 loss away to the same opponents.

"My players suffered deep psychological trauma due to their helplessness," lamented Romulo Cortez, the Maldives coach.

Such is the adventure of the World Cup and such the all-encompassing arms of the tournament that The Maldives will almost certainly be back. Football is a game that is forever crossing frontiers and from 13 countries entering the first competition in 1930, it has grown and grown. By 1958, 53 teams were challenging for the right to be in the

finals in Sweden, by Argentina in 1978 it was 106, for the USA in 1994 it was 144 and now 170. There seems to be no limit.

The beauty of the game is the common language it creates to unite all people; whether sharing a social sheep's eyeball or two in Tunis or a pint of heavy in Edinburgh, there are extraordinary World Cup stories to be shared. England's real World Cup hero is Pickles the dog. Had the aforementioned mongrel not gone sniffing in some bushes in a park in Norwood, south London, the famous Jules Rimet trophy, which had been stolen from an exhibition in central London, might not have been in place to be presented to Bobby Moore, England's 1966 World Cup-winning captain. Pickles, as his reward, was invited to the celebration banquet and allowed to lick the plates clean.

On a more prosaic note, it was not until 1974 that the Final had a penalty - and then it had two in the first half. West Germany were playing Holland in Munich and the match was less than a minute old when Johan Cruyff was clattered in the penalty box. Johan Neeskens scored to record the quickest goal in a Final and to boot, the Germans were to have their first kick of the ball in the match from the restart. They were to get their own penalty 25 minutes later. Just to add more spice to an eventful day, the start to the game was delayed after Jack Taylor, the English referee, noticed there were no corner flags.

And like those penalties, it is astonishing to discover that a World Cup Final did not produce a goalscoring captain until 1970 when Carlos Alberto, one of the greatest defenders of any generation, delivered the coup de grace as Brazil won the Jules Rimet trophy for keeps (it was

Below: Victory for
Scotland over Estonia
after three seconds!
Bottom: Maradona and
the infamous 'Hand of
God' goal.
Opposite: Cruyff is
felled in the first
minute for a Dutch
penalty and a 1-0 lead
in the 1974 Final.

later to be stolen and never seen again)
when they thrashed Italy 4-1 in Mexico.
In the process, their coach Mario Zagalo
became the first man to play for and
manage a winning side and Jairzinho
was the first player to score in every
round of the finals. However, he did not
win the tournament's Golden Boot for
being the most prolific striker, that
honour going to West Germany's
Gerhard Muller with 10 goals.

In terms of the record book, 1982 in
Spain was to be a watershed year. Laszlo
Kiss became the first substitute to score a
hat-trick as Hungary produced a finals'
best win, 10-1, over El Salvador while
England celebrated the fastest goal in the
finals - 27 seconds - scored by Bryan
Robson in a 3-1 win over France. The
penalty, a tool used increasingly in the
game, made a first shoot-out appearance
when West Germany beat France 5-4
after a 3-3 draw, while Antonio Cabrini,
of Italy, had the dubious honour of
becoming the first player to miss a
penalty in the Final.

Every qualifying group, every finals is
littered with such adventures and
surprise. We know France 1998 is the
biggest and most expensive World Cup
yet, the most cosmopolitan and with the
largest-ever TV audience. Yet playing
before massed ranks, either there at the
ground or glued before the TV set, is
never guaranteed - not even for the
greatest tournament on earth.

When Scotland went to face Estonia in
October 1997, they ran out into a
virtually deserted stadium, won the toss,
kicked off and seconds later heard the
whistle blow to signal the end of the
match. The reason? Estonia had not
turned up. FIFA had ruled the floodlights
were not up to standard for a World Cup
qualifier and ordered the kick-off to be
brought forward - only somehow the
Estonians didn't get the message and
didn't show. In the end it was all
resolved even though Scotland, having
initially been awarded the game, were
made to replay it and could only manage
a 0-0 draw.

As for more tales of the expected for
France - Brazil to dazzle, Alan Shearer to
score, France to do well.

The tales of the unexpected - Iran to be
crowned winners, touts to give away
their tickets for free and Peter Shilton to
receive a surprise call-up for England. It
couldn't happen, could it?

Unlikely, but possible, the element of the
unexpected is at the core of our
fascination with the game and if the
"Hand of God" can make such a visible
contribution as it did in the finals of
Mexico City 1986, then who knows
what divine inspiration or intervention
will be on show in France?

ENGLAND IN THE WORLD CUP By Brian Glanville

Football correspondent of The Times and the doyen of the World's Press boxes, he has covered eleven World Cup finals and is the author of the definitive history, 'The Story of the World Cup'

England could scarcely have made a more calamitous start in the World Cup. Beaten in Brazil by the United States, then a conglomeration of local league players and obscure foreigners, among them a Scottish skipper and right-half called Eddie McIlvenny, who had not long since been given a free transfer by Wrexham of the Third Division North. England had qualified for the Brazilian finals of 1950 - their absence in previous World Cups determined by their resigning from FIFA - thanks to leading the British International Championship. They beat Chile in Rio, but a team full of great stars - Tom Finney, Wilf Mannion, Alf Ramsey, Stan Mortensen, Billy Wright - just couldn't score against an American team both resilient and fortunate. The only goal was headed in by a Haitian centre-forward, Joe Gaetjens; later a victim of Tons Tons Macoute. A second defeat by Spain in Rio and England were out. They qualified again in 1954, for Switzerland, and did better. Thirty-nine-year-old Stanley Matthews, who'd played against Spain in 1950, had a marvellous match in Basel against Belgium, switching from right wing to inside forward, but the result was a 4-4 draw. After beating the Swiss in Berne 2-0, England came up against the holders Uruguay in the quarter-finals in Basel. Uruguay had beaten the Scots 7-0. England, with Matthews exceptional again and Billy Wright formidable in his new role as centre-half, gave them a much closer game, but Gil Merrick's weak goalkeeping and Juan Schiaffino's brilliance enabled Uruguay to win 4-2; though one goal came when skipper Obdulio Varela took a dropped-ball free kick. England's 1958 participation in Sweden was overshadowed by the appalling Munich air disaster which took so many young Manchester United players' lives, among them three key men in left-back Roger Byrne, driving left-half Duncan Edwards and centre-forward Tommy Taylor. Astonishingly, England didn't even take their full complement of 22 players with them, leaving such as Nat Lofthouse and Stanley Matthews behind. In their first game, a narrowly achieved 2-2 draw with the USSR in Gothenburg, another star, Tom Finney, was injured and out. Two more draws followed, an impressive 0-0 against powerful Brazil (though no Pele), an untidy 2-2 against Austria. In the resulting play-off, England inexplicably threw in two debutants, Peter Broadbent and Peter Brabrook, at the deep end, continued to ignore Bobby Charlton, and lost 1-0 to the USSR.

In 1962, England were competing again in Chile, managed for the fourth and last time by academic Walter Winterbottom. At the little copper company stadium in Rancagua, England and Bobby Charlton played well to defeat Argentina, the midfield strengthened by the emergence of 21-year-old half-back Bobby Moore. But dull draws against Hungary and Bulgaria were ill omens and, in the quarter-final at Vina del Mar, the explosive skills of Garrincha were irresistible. Small though he was, he even headed a goal from a corner. England went out 3-1. World Cup 1966 saw the finals played in England for the only time so far. Now England had a truly inspirational manager in Alf Ramsey, one who insisted on full control. His players worshipped him. England, he swore, would win the World Cup, but they began at Wembley - where all their games were played - with an uneasy 0-0 draw against Uruguay. The fulminating shooting of Bobby Charlton, now their deep-lying centre-forward, brought 2-0 victory against Mexico and one by the same score against France. In the quarter-finals, England came up against a bruising Argentina team which littered the match with petty fouls. Eventually, the German referee, Herr Kreitlein, sent off the Argentina captain, towering Antonio Rattin, 'for the look on his face', but with Roma acrobatic in goal, England still found it so hard to score. They won finally through a superb header by Geoff Hurst, the muscular West Ham striker, brought in for his first World Cup game. The cross came from another accomplished West Ham man,

Golden boot winner
Gary Lineker in action
against Paraguay in
the 1986 World Cup.

England's finest hour
as Bobby Moore holds
aloft the 1966
World Cup trophy.

Gascoigne went from
strength to strength in
Italia '90 – to no avail.
England eventually
lost out to Germany on
penalties in the
semi-finals.

midfielder Martin Peters. Ramsey was now playing without wingers. In the semi-final, England came good at last, Bobby Charlton scoring twice against Portugal and Nobby Stiles, the battling little Manchester United half-back, subduing the prolific Eusebio. Portugal rallied and scored from a late penalty. 2-1. In the Final against West Germany, Bobby Charlton and 21-year-old Franz Beckenbauer virtually cancelled each other out. A wayward header by left-back Ray Wilson enabled Helmut Haller to put the Germans ahead, but inspired by a superb Bobby Moore, whose free kick gave Hurst the equaliser, England led 2-1 when Peters scored. But at the death, the Germans equalised. Some thought the free kick should have gone to Jackie Charlton rather than against him. Lothar Emmerich drove it against Karl-Heinz Schnellinger's back, the ball eventually reaching Weber, who made it 2-2. Hurst in extra time scored the most controversial of all World Cup goals. Alan Ball, irresistible on the right flank, crossed, Hurst drove against the underside of the bar, the Swiss referee Dienst consulted his linesman, Bakhramov . . . and he gave the goal. In the final seconds, Moore sent Hurst through for his third. Mexico 1970 saw England and Ramsey make a brave bid. Had that superb goalkeeper Gordon Banks not fallen ill before the quarter-final at Leon, would England have reached the Final?

In Guadalajara, England beat a rough Romania, then lost 1-0 to Brazil in a thrilling game distinguished by Banks' amazing one-handed save from a Pele header. A foul on Bobby Moore helped Brazil's goal, Jeff Astle missed a sitter for England. In Leon, at dizzy height and in fearsome noonday heat, England began so well against West Germany, taking a two-goal lead, right-half Alan Mullery creator and scorer of the first. But the reserve 'keeper Peter Bonetti looked rusty, Franz Beckenbauer equalised, Alf Ramsey inexplicably pulled off Bobby Charlton and the tide turned, Uwe Seeler, with a freakish backheader, and Gerd Muller scoring for the Germans with the English full-backs wilting in the heat. England failed to qualify in 1974 and 1978, but were unbeaten in five matches in the 1982 tournament in Spain. Would they have gone to the Final had manager Ron Greenwood not been persuaded to use a clearly below-par Kevin Keegan in the vital last game against Spain in Madrid? Keegan, who came on as a substitute, missed a simple headed chance, England drew 0-0 as they'd previously done against West Germany in this Group B second round, and thus were eliminated, a point behind the Germans. They'd won all their games in Group 4. An instant goal by Bryan Robson in Bilbao had unsettled France, Robson got another, England won 3-1. With the lithe, gifted Trevor Francis exploiting Glenn Hoddle's searching long passes, the Czechs were beaten 2-0; Kuwait, somewhat laboriously, were defeated 1-0. Had West

> '**Had Gordon Banks not fallen ill before the quarter-final at Leon, would we have reached the final?**'

Ham's influential playmaker Trevor Brooking been fit, had Glenn Hoddle been used against Germany, had Ron Greenwood not been so over-cautious, perhaps England would have won that game. As it was, they went out, unbeaten but uninspiring, Greenwood exulting in the fact that they hadn't allowed the German right-back, Manny Kaltz, to get in any crosses! In 1986, they were undermined in their second-round match against Argentina in Mexico City by Diego Maradona's Hand-of-God goal - blatantly punched against Peter Shilton, but given by an inept linesman and referee. England had started abysmally against Portugal - a drab defeat - and Morocco. Incomprehensible was the manager Bobby Robson's insistence on playing his namesake, Bryan, though his dislocated shoulder kept going out. After the edgy draw with Morocco in Monterrey, there was virtually a rebellion by several England players. Bryan Robson dropped out, square-passing Ray Wilkins was suspended, and the verve of Gary Lineker (tournament leading scorer), Peter Reid and Peter Beardsley brought fine victories against Poland and sometimes brutal Paraguay. Maradona followed his punched goal with a glorious solo goal. The late arrival of John Barnes galvanised England but his left-flank raid brought only a single goal, by Lineker. In 1990, England went further, going out against West Germany in the semi-final only on penalties; always such a blight on a World Cup. They were poor in their drawn opening game in Cagliari against Ireland, but with Paul Gascoigne going from strength to strength in midfield, a creative force. Pressed by his players, Bobby Robson used a sweeper against Holland in Mark Wright and drew honourably. Wright then headed the only goal against Egypt. England were back to 4-4-2, but Wright was sweeper again against surprising Cameroon in Naples until he was injured. 'A flat back four saved us,' said Bobby Robson next day. It did. Paul Parker marked the ebullient veteran Roger Milla and England, who had gone behind 2-1, levelled to 2-2 and then prevailed in extra time through a couple of penalties by Lineker. Nor should one forget the superbly volleyed goal by David Platt in Bologna against Belgium, which had got them thus far. In Turin, Terry Butcher played sweeper and West Germany looked tired, but they went ahead after 59 minutes when Brehme's shot hit Parker and looped over Shilton. An unmarked Lineker equalised, but missed penalties by Stuart Pearce and Chris Waddle sealed England's fate. England failed to land the trip to the States in 1994, but this time Glenn Hoddle's team starts among the favourites. It should certainly qualify from its group and looks good enough to survive the next round - even against the talented Croatia. The semi-finals should be within reach but Brazil stand in the way of ultimate victory.

THE HIGHS AND LOWS OF

1950

BRAZIL

KEY: Q – QUALIFYING **F** – FINALS
NOS IN BRACKETS – GOALS SCORED
NAMES IN BRACKETS – SUBSTITUTES

Q. Wales (a) won 4-1: Williams, Mozley, Aston, W Wright capt, Franklin, Dickinson, Finney, Mortensen (1), Milburn (3), Shackleton, Hancocks.

Q. Northern Ireland (h) won 9-2: Streten, Mozley, Aston, W Watson, Franklin, W Wright capt, Finney, Mortensen (2), J Rowley (4), Pearson (2), J Froggatt (1).

Q. Scotland (a) won 1-0: Williams, Ramsey, Aston, W Wright capt, Franklin, Dickinson, Finney, Mannion, Mortensen, Bentley (1), Langton.

F. Chile won 2-0: Williams, Ramsey, Aston, W Wright capt, L Hughes, Dickinson, Finney, Mannion (1), Bentley, Mortensen (1), Mullen.

F. USA lost 0-1: Williams, Ramsey, Aston, W Wright capt, L Hughes, Dickinson, Finney, Mannion, Bentley, Mortensen, Mullen.

F. Spain lost 0-1: Williams, Ramsey, Eckersley, W Wright capt, L Hughes, Dickinson, S Matthews, Mortensen, Milburn, E Baily, Finney.

Fifties stars, Stanley Matthews and (opposite) skipper Billy Wright

ENGLAND'S CUP DREAMS

1954

SWITZERLAND

Q. Wales (a) won 4-1: Merrick, Garrett, Eckersley, W Wright capt, Johnston, Dickinson, Finney, Quixall, Lofthouse (2), Wilshaw (2), Mullen.

Q. Northern Ireland (h) won 3-1: Merrick, Rickaby, Eckersley, W Wright capt, Johnston, Dickinson, S Matthews, Quixall, Lofthouse (1), Hassall (2), Mullen.

Q. Scotland (a) won 4-2: Merrick, Staniforth, R Byrne, W Wright capt, H Clarke, Dickinson, Finney, Broadis (1), R Allen (1), Nicholls (1), Mullen (1).

F. Belgium draw 4-4: Merrick, Staniforth, R Byrne, W Wright capt, Owen, Dickinson, S Matthews, Broadis (2), Lofthouse (2), T Taylor, Finney.

F. Switzerland won 2-0: Merrick, Staniforth, R Byrne, McGarry, W Wright capt, Dickinson, Finney, Broadis, T Taylor, Wilshaw (1), Mullen (1).

F. Uruguay lost 2-4: Merrick, Staniforth, R Byrne, McGarry, W Wright capt, Dickinson, S Matthews, Broadis, Lofthouse (1), Wilshaw, Finney (1).

1958

SWEDEN

Q. Denmark (h) won 5-2: Ditchburn, Hall, R Byrne, Clayton, W Wright capt, Dickinson, S Matthews, Brooks, T Taylor (3), Edwards (2), Finney.

Q. Eire (h) won 5-1: Hodgkinson, Hall, R Byrne, Clayton, W Wright capt, Edwards, S Matthews, Atyeo (2), T Taylor (3), Haynes, Finney.

Q. Denmark (a) won 4-1: Hodgkinson, Hall, R Byrne, Clayton, W Wright capt, Edwards, S Matthews, Atyeo (1), T Taylor (2), Haynes (1), Finney.

Q. Eire (a) draw 1-1: Hodgkinson, Hall, R Byrne, Clayton, W Wright capt, Edwards, Finney, Atyeo (1), T Taylor, Haynes, Pegg.

F. Soviet Union draw 2-2: McDonald, D Howe, T Banks, Clamp, W Wright capt, Slater, Douglas, R Robson, Kevan (1), Haynes, Finney (1).

F. Brazil draw 0-0: McDonald, D Howe, T Banks, Clamp, W Wright capt, Slater, Douglas, R Robson, Kevan, Haynes, A'Court.

F. Austria draw 2-2: McDonald, D Howe, T Banks, Clamp, W Wright capt, Slater, Douglas, R Robson, Kevan (1), Haynes (1), A'Court.

F. Soviet Union lost 0-1: McDonald, D Howe, T Banks, Clayton, W Wright capt, Slater, Brabrook, Broadbent, Kevan, Haynes, A'Court.

1962

CHILE

Q. Luxembourg (a) won 9-0: R Springett, Armfield, McNeil, R Robson, Swan, R Flowers, Douglas, Greaves (3), R Smith (2), Haynes capt (1), R Charlton (3).

Q. Portugal (a) draw 1-1: R Springett, Armfield, McNeil, R Robson, Swan, R Flowers (1), Douglas, Greaves, R Smith, Haynes capt, R Charlton.

Q. Luxembourg (h) won 4-1: R Springett, Armfield capt, McNeil, R Robson, Swan, R Flowers, Douglas, Fantham, Pointer (1), Viollet (1), R Charlton (2).

Q. Portugal (h) won 2-0: R Springett, Armfield, Wilson, R Robson, Swan, R Flowers,

Connelly (1), Douglas, Pointer (1), Haynes capt, R Charlton.

F. Hungary lost 1-2; R Springett, Armfield, Wilson, Moore, Norman, R Flowers (1), Douglas, Greaves, Hitchens, Haynes capt, R Charlton.

F. Argentina won 3-1: R Springett, Armfield, Wilson, Moore, Norman, R Flowers (1), Douglas, Greaves (1), Peacock, Haynes capt, R Charlton (1).

F. Bulgaria draw 0-0: R Springett, Armfield, Wilson, Moore, Norman, R Flowers, Douglas, Greaves, Peacock, Haynes capt, R Charlton.

F. Brazil lost 1-3: R Springett, Armfield, Wilson, Moore, Norman, R Flowers, Douglas, Greaves, Hitchens (1), Haynes capt, R Charlton.

1966

ENGLAND

F. Uruguay draw 0-0: G Banks, Cohen, Wilson, Stiles, J Charlton, Moore capt, Ball, Greaves, R Charlton, Hunt, Connelly.

F. Mexico won 2-0: G Banks, Cohen, Wilson, Stiles, J Charlton, Moore capt, Paine, Greaves, R Charlton (1), Hunt (1), Peters.

F. France won 2-0: G Banks, Cohen, Wilson, Stiles, J Charlton, Moore capt, Callaghan, Greaves, R Charlton, Hunt (2), Peters.

F. Argentina won 1-0: G Banks, Cohen, Wilson, Stiles, J Charlton, Moore capt, Ball, Hurst (1), R Charlton, Hunt, Peters.

F. Portugal won 2-1: G Banks, Cohen, Wilson, Stiles, J Charlton, Moore capt, Ball, Hurst, R Charlton (2), Hunt, Peters.

F. West Germany won 4-2: G Banks, Cohen, Wilson, Stiles, J Charlton, Moore capt, Ball, Hurst (3), R Charlton, Hunt, Peters (1).

A grand and glorious moment from the England picture book as Martin Peters makes it 2-1 with barely ten minutes to go. It looked to be all over before West Germany's late equaliser – and the agony of extra time. Opposite: On-the-spot attention for the flattened Pele, victim of many tough tackles in his four World Cup finals. Below: Action man Bobby Charlton, star of 106 matches and 49 goals for England.

1970

MEXICO

F. Romania won 1-0: G Banks, Newton (T Wright), Cooper, Mullery, Labone, Moore capt, F Lee (Osgood), Ball, R Charlton, Hurst (1), Peters.

F. Brazil lost 0-1: G Banks, T Wright, Cooper, Mullery, Labone, Moore capt, F Lee (Astle), Ball, R Charlton (Bell), Hurst Peters.

F. Czechoslovakia won 1-0: G Banks, Newton, Cooper, Mullery, J Charlton, Moore capt, Bell, R Charlton (Ball), Astle, A Clarke (1) (Osgood), Peters.

F. West Germany lost 2-3: Bonetti, Newton, Cooper, Mullery (1), Labone, Moore capt, F Lee, Ball, R Charlton (Bell), Hurst, Peters (1) (Hunter).

1974

WEST GERMANY

Q. Wales (a) won 1-0: Clemence, Storey, E Hughes, Hunter, McFarland, Moore capt, Keegan, Chivers, Marsh, Bell (1), Ball.

Q. Wales (h) draw 1-1: Clemence, Storey, E Hughes, Hunter (1), McFarland, Moore capt, Keegan, Bell, Chivers. Marsh, Ball.

Q. Poland (a) lost 0-2: Shilton, Madeley, E Hughes, Storey, McFarland, Moore capt, Ball, Bell, Chivers, A Clarke, Peters.

Q. Poland (h) draw 1-1: Shilton, Madeley, E Hughes, Bell, McFarland, Hunter, Currie, Channon, Chivers (Hector), A Clarke (1), Peters capt.

Mutual admiration in Mexico as Bobby Moore and Pele exchange shirts and compliments after the Brazil-England clash. Below: A rare shot of another pair of all-time greats, Johan Cruyff and Franz Beckenbauer. Right: The supreme moment for Italy in Madrid, and despair for West Germany, as the final whistle sounds in the 1982 Final. Below right: Argentina's captain Daniel Passarella after the 1978 Final victory in Buenos Aires over Holland.

1978

ARGENTINA

Q. Finland (a) won 4-1: Clemence, Todd, Mills, Phil Thompson, Madeley, Cherry, Keegan (2), Channon (1), Pearson (1), Brooking, G Francis capt.

Q. Luxembourg (h) won 5-0: Clemence, Gidman, Cherry, R Kennedy (1), Dave Watson (1974-82), E Hughes, Keegan capt (1), Channon (2), Royle (Mariner), T Francis (1), Hill.

Q. Luxembourg (a) won 2-0: Clemence, Cherry, Watson (Beattie), E Hughes capt, Kennedy (1), Callaghan, McDermott (Whymark), Wilkins, T Francis, Mariner (1), Hill.

Q. Italy (h) won 2-0: Clemence, Neal, Cherry, Wilkins, Watson, E Hughes capt (T Francis), Keegan (1), Coppell, Latchford (Pearson), Brooking (1), P Barnes.

Q. Finland (h) won 2-1: Clemence, Todd, Beattie, P Thompson, Greenhoff, Wilkins, Keegan capt, Channon, Royle (1), Brooking (Mills), Tueart (1) (G Hill).

Q. Italy (a) lost 0-2: Clemence, Clement (Beattie), Mills, Greenhoff, McFarland, E Hughes, Keegan capt, Channon, Bowles, Cherry, Brooking.

1982

SPAIN

Q. Norway (h) won 4-0: Shilton, Anderson, Sansom, P Thompson capt, Watson, B Robson, Gates, McDermott (2), Mariner (1), Woodcock (1), Rix.

Q. Romania (a) lost 1-2: Clemence, Neal, Sansom, P Thompson capt, Watson, Robson, Rix, McDermott, Birtles (Cunningham), Woodcock (1), Gates (Coppell).

Q. Switzerland (h) won 2-1: Shilton, Neal, Sansom, Robson, Watson, Mills capt, Coppell, McDermott, Mariner (1), Brooking (Rix), Woodcock. (One own goal).

Q. Romania (h) draw 0-0: Shilton, Anderson, Samson, Robson, Watson capt, Osman, Wilkins, Brooking, Coppell, T Francis, Woodcock (McDermott).

Q. Switzerland (a) lost 1-2: Clemence, Mills, Samson, Wilkins, Watson (P Barnes), Osman, Keegan capt, Robson, Coppell, Mariner, T Francis (McDermott).

Q. Hungary (a) won 3-1: Clemence, Neal, Mills, Thompson, Watson, Robson, Keegan capt (1), McDermott, Mariner, Brooking (2) (Wilkins), Coppell.

Q. Norway (a) lost 1-2: Clemence, Neal, Mills, Thompson, Osman, Robson (1), Keegan capt, T Francis, Mariner (Withe), Hoddle (P Barnes), McDermott.

Q. Hungary (h) won 1-0: Shilton, Neal, Mills, Thompson, Martin, Robson, Keegan capt, Coppell (Morley), Mariner (1), Brooking, McDermott.

F. France won 3-1: Shilton, Mills capt, Sansom (Neal), Thompson, Butcher, Robson (2), Coppell, T Francis, Mariner (1), Rix, Wilkins.

F. Czechoslovakia won 2-0: Shilton, Mills capt, Sansom, Thompson, Butcher, Robson (Hoddle), Coppell, T Francis (1), Mariner, Rix, Wilkins. (One own goal).

F. Kuwait won 1-0: Shilton, Neal, Mills capt, Thompson, Foster, Hoddle, Coppell, T Francis (1), Mariner, Rix, Wilkins.

F. West Germany draw 0-0: Shilton, Mills capt, Sansom, Thompson, Butcher, Robson, Coppell, T Francis (Woodcock), Mariner, Rix, Wilkins.

F. Spain draw 0-0: Shilton, Mills capt, Sansom, Thompson, Butcher, Robson, Rix (Brooking), T Francis, Mariner, Woodcock (Keegan), Wilkins.

1986

MEXICO

Q. Finland (h) won 5-0: Shilton, Duxbury (G A Stevens,Tottenham), Sansom (1), Williams, M Wright, Butcher, Robson capt (1) (Chamberlain), Wilkins, Hateley (2), Woodcock (1),J Barnes.

Q. Turkey (a) won 8-0: Shilton, Anderson (1), Sansom, Williams (G Λ Stevens), Wright, Butcher, Robson capt (3), Wilkins, Withe, Woodcock (2) (Francis) Barnes (2).

Q. Northern Ireland (a) won 1-0: Shilton, Anderson, Sansom, Steven, Martin, Butcher, Stevens (Everton & Rangers), Wilkins capt, Hateley (1), Woodcock (Francis), Barnes.

Q. Romania (a) draw 0-0: Shilton, Anderson, Sansom, Steven, Wright, Butcher, Robson capt, Wilkins, Mariner (Lineker), Francis, Barnes (Waddle).

Q. Finland (a) draw 1-1: Shilton, Anderson, Sansom, Steven (Waddle), Fenwick, Butcher, Robson capt, Wilkins, Hateley (1), Francis, Barnes.

Q. Romania (h) draw 1-1: Shilton, Stevens, Sansom, Reid, Wright, Fenwick, Robson capt, Hoddle (1), Hateley, Lineker (Woodcock), Waddle (Barnes)

Q. Turkey (h) won 5-0: Shilton, Stevens, Sansom, Hoddle, Wright, Fenwick, Robson capt (1) (Steven), Wilkins, Hateley (Woodcock), Lineker (3), Waddle (1).

Q. Northern Ireland (h) draw 0-0: Shilton, G A Stevens, Sansom, Hoddle, Wright, Fenwick, Bracewell, Wilkins capt, K Dixon, Lineker, Waddle.

F. Portugal lost 0-1: Shilton, Stevens, Sansom, Hoddle, Fenwick, Butcher, Robson capt (Hodge), Wilkins, Hateley, Lineker, Waddle (Beardsley).

F. Morocco draw 0-0: Shilton, Stevens, Sansom, Hoddle, Fenwick, Butcher, Robson capt (Hodge), Wilkins, Hateley (G A Stevens), Lineker, Waddle.

F. Poland won 3-0: Shilton capt, Stevens, Sansom, Hoddle, Fenwick, Butcher, Hodge, Reid, Beardsley (Waddle), Lineker (3) (Dixon), Steven.

F. Paraguay won 3-0: Shilton capt, Stevens, Sansom, Hoddle, Martin, Butcher, Hodge, Reid (G A Stevens), Beardsley (1) (Hateley), Lineker (2), Steven.

F. Argentina lost 1-2: Shilton capt, Stevens, Sansom, Hoddle, Fenwick, Butcher, Hodge, Reid (Waddle), Beardsley, Lineker (1), Steven (Barnes).

1990

ITALY

Q. Sweden (h) draw 0-0: Shilton, Stevens, Pearce, Webb, Adams (Walker), Butcher, Robson capt, Beardsley, Waddle, Lineker, Barnes (Cottee).

Q. Albania (a) won 2-0: Shilton, Stevens, Pearce, Webb, Walker, Butcher, Robson capt (1), Rocastle, Waddle (Beardsley), Lineker (A Smith), Barnes (1).

Q. Albania (h) won 5-0: Shilton, Stevens (Parker), Pearce, Webb, Walker, Butcher, Robson capt, Rocastle (Gascoigne 1), Beardsley (2), Lineker (1), Waddle (1).

Q. Poland (h) won 3-0: Shilton, Stevens, Pearce, Webb (1), Walker, Butcher, Robson capt, Waddle (Rocastle), Beardsley (A Smith), Lineker (1), Barnes (1).

Q. Sweden (a) draw 0-0: Shilton, Stevens, Pearce, Webb (Gascoigne), Walker, Butcher capt, Beardsley, McMahon, Waddle, Lineker, Barnes (Rocastle).

Q. Poland (a) draw 0-0: Shilton, Stevens, Pearce, McMahon, Walker, Butcher, Robson capt, Rocastle, Beardsley, Lineker, Waddle.

F. Eire draw 1-1: Shilton, Stevens, Pearce, Gascoigne, Walker, Butcher, Waddle, Robson capt, Beardsley (McMahon), Lineker (1) (Bull), Barnes.

F. Holland draw 0-0: Shilton, Parker, Pearce, Wright, Walker, Butcher, Robson capt (Platt), Waddle (Bull), Gascoigne, Lineker, Barnes.

F. Egypt won 1-0: Shilton capt, Parker, Pearce, Gascoigne, Walker, Wright (1), McMahon, Waddle (Platt), Bull (Beardsley), Lineker, Barnes.

F. Belgium won 1-0: Shilton, Parker, Pearce, Wright, Walker, Butcher capt, McMahon (Platt 1), Waddle, Gascoigne, Lineker, Barnes (Bull).

F. Cameroon won 3-2: Shilton, Parker, Pearce, Wright, Walker, Butcher capt (Steven), Platt (1), Waddle, Gascoigne, Lineker (2), Barnes (Beardsley).

F. West Germany draw 1-1: Shilton, Parker, Pearce, Wright, Walker, Butcher capt (Steven), Platt, Waddle, Gascoigne, Lineker (1), Beardsley.

F. Italy lost 1-2: Shilton capt, Stevens, Dorigo, Parker, Walker, Wright (Waddle), Platt (1), Steven, McMahon (Webb), Lineker, Beardsley.

Gary Lineker on target against West Germany in Italy 1990, but England went down in the shoot-out. He's there again (opposite) with No 2 in his hat-trick against Poland in Mexico 1986.

1994
USA

Q. Norway (h) draw 1-1: Woods, L Dixon (Palmer), Pearce capt, Batty, Walker, Adams, Platt (1), Gascoigne, Shearer, I Wright (Merson), Ince.

Q. Turkey (h) won 4-0: Woods, Dixon, Pearce capt (1), Palmer, Walker, Adams, Platt, Gascoigne (2), Shearer (1), I Wright, Ince.

Q. San Marino (h) won 6-0: Woods, Dixon, Dorigo, Palmer (1), Walker, Adams, Platt capt (4), Gascoigne, Ferdinand (1), Barnes, Batty.

Q. Turkey (a) won 2-0: Woods, Dixon (Clough), Sinton, Palmer, Walker, Adams, Platt capt (1), Gascoigne (1), Barnes, I Wright (Sharpe), Ince.

Q. Holland (h) draw 2-2: Woods, Dixon, Keown, Palmer, Walker, Adams, Platt capt (1), Gascoigne (Merson), Ferdinand, Barnes (1), Ince.

Q. Poland (a) draw 1-1: Woods, Bardsley, Dorigo, Palmer (I Wright 1), Walker, Adams, Platt capt, Gascoigne (Clough), Sheringham, Barnes, Ince.

Q. Norway (a) lost 0-2: Woods, Dixon, Pallister, Palmer, Walker (Clough), Adams, Platt capt, Gascoigne, Ferdinand, Sheringham (I Wright), Sharpe.

Q. Poland (h) won 3-0: Seaman, Jones, Pearce capt (1), Ince, Pallister, Adams, Platt, Gascoigne (1), Ferdinand (1), I Wright, Sharpe.

Q. Holland (a) lost 0-2: Seaman, Parker, Dorigo, Ince, Pallister, Adams, Platt capt, Palmer (Sinton), Shearer, Merson (I Wright), Sharpe.

Q. San Marino (a) won 7-1: Seaman, Dixon, Pearce capt, Ince (2), Pallister, Walker, Platt, Ripley, Ferdinand (1), I Wright (4), Sinton.

England are on the way to a 7-1 win over San Marino, so why the gloom? Because it's all over in 1994 and there's no trip to the States.

1998
FRANCE

Q. Moldova (a) won 3-0: Seaman, G Neville, Pearce, Ince, Pallister, Southgate, Beckham, Gascoigne (1) (Batty), Shearer capt (1), Barmby (1) (Le Tissier), Hinchcliffe.

Q. Poland (h) won 2-1: Seaman, G Neville, Pearce, Ince, Southgate (Pallister), Hinchcliffe, Beckham, Gascoigne, Shearer capt (2), Ferdinand, McManaman.

Q. Georgia (a) won 2-0: Seaman, Campbell, Hinchcliffe, Ince, Adams capt, Southgate, Beckham, Gascoigne, Ferdinand (1) (I Wright), Sheringham (1), Batty.

Q. Italy (h) lost 0-1: Walker, G Neville, Pearce, Ince, Campbell, Le Saux, Beckham, Batty (I Wright), Shearer capt, Le Tissier (Ferdinand), McManaman (Merson).

Q. Georgia (h) won 2-0: Seaman, G Neville, Campbell, Batty, Adams (Southgate), Le Saux, Beckham, Ince (Redknapp), Shearer capt (1), Sheringham (1), Lee.

Q. Poland (a) won 2-0: Seaman, G Neville, Campbell, Ince, Southgate, Le Saux, Beckham (P Neville), Gascoigne (Batty), Shearer capt (1), Sheringham (1), Lee.

Q. Moldova (h) won 4-0: Seaman capt, G Neville, Campbell, Southgate, P Neville, Beckham (Ripley, Butt), Batty, Gascoigne (1), Scholes (1), Ferdinand (Collymore), I Wright (2).

Q. Italy (a) draw 0-0: Seaman, Campbell, Southgate, Adams, Le Saux, Beckham, Ince capt, Batty, Gascoigne (Butt), I Wright, Sheringham.